Wolf and the Winds

Wolf and the Winds

By Frank Bird Linderman

INTRODUCTION BY HUGH A. DEMPSEY

UNIVERSITY OF OKLAHOMA PRESS : NORMAN AND LONDON

Also by Frank Bird Linderman

Recollections of Charley Russell (edited by H. G. Merriam; Norman,
1963, 1984)

Library of Congress Cataloging-in-Publication Data

Linderman, Frank Bird, 1869–1938.
  Wolf and the winds.

  Includes bibliographical references.
  1. Atsina Indians—Fiction.   2. Montana—History—
Fiction.   I. Title.
PS3523.I535W65   1986   813'.52   86–40075
ISBN 0–8061–2007–x (alk. paper)

The paper in this book meets the guidelines for permanence and
durability of the Committee on Production Guidelines for Book
Longevity of the Council on Library Resources.

Contents

Introduction

HUGH A. DEMPSEY

This volume joins fourteen other books written by Montana author Frank Bird Linderman published between 1915 and 1935. Most of the others were Indian legends or works of nonfiction; only *Lige Mounts, Free Trapper* and *Beyond Law* were novels.

Like George Bird Grinnell and James Willard Schultz, Linderman is best known and remembered for his books about Indians. His monumental work, *American: The Life Story of a Great Indian, Plenty-Coups, Chief of the Crows*, has been for many years an American classic.

In some ways Linderman was an unlikely candidate to become an author of Indian stories. His career as an assayer, politician, and salesman would seem to have been far removed from smoke-filled tipis and book-lined studies. Yet his interest in Indians began early in life, and his tendency toward writing, though almost accidental, became a perfect outlet for his creativity and need to record the lives and experiences of American Indians.

Frank Bird Linderman was born in Cleveland, Ohio, on September 25, 1869, and later moved with his family to

Chicago. From as early as he could remember, he was fascinated by the West, and at the age of sixteen, after studying a large map, he was determined to become a trapper in the Flathead Lake region of western Montana. His parents, after some discussion, decided to let him get the wanderlust out of his system; perhaps that was a mistake, for Linderman never returned home. The Flathead Lake region became his Mecca, his lifetime goal for a permanent wilderness haven.

In launching his western adventure, Linderman persuaded a schoolmate and the boy's coachman, who had served in the West in the army, to join him. After traveling by train, steamboat, and bobsled, in March, 1885, they finally arrived in Flathead country where they built a crude trapper's cabin. At this point Linderman's two companions decided they had had enough of wilderness life and fled to the comforts of Chicago. But the young adventurer remained and, Flathead Indians and local frontiersmen taught him how to survive in the wilds. For the next five years he learned how to trap, to fear the warlike Kootenais, and to depend on the more friendly Flatheads. He soon came to know the wilderness, the animals, and the freedom that the life offered. He also felt a kinship and sympathy for the Indians, who were gradually being forced back or corrupted by the onslaught of civilization.

In 1890, Linderman met Minnie Jane Johns, and when he decided to marry her, he realized that he would have to give up his carefree life as a trapper. Recalling an offer of help from Montana Governor Sam Hauser, whom he had guided on a hunting expedition, Linderman sought him out in Missoula. This led to a temporary job as watchman at a mine, and, while there, he began to learn assaying. This in turn took him to an assaying position in Butte. In that town he became involved in politics, serving as delegate to the Republican county convention.

In 1896 he had become tired of Butte, so he moved to the tiny community of Sheridan, where he opened his own assay office and became increasingly involved in politics. But three years of near starvation for him and his family finally caused him to make a plunge into an entirely new field. In 1899 he purchased the local newspaper, the *Sheridan Chinook*, and found that he had a natural flair for writing. To fill up space in the paper, he started a column, "Seen at the Corner," and began to sprinkle his own stories and poems among the news items. Within a short time writing had become an important part of his life.

Four years later he was elected to the Montana State Legislature as the representative for Madison County. In addition, from 1905 to 1907 he was the assistant secretary of state and for a time was acting secretary of state. As he joined the bitter infighting of Montana politics, his interest in Indians became well known, and his own pressure group was dubbed "the Indians." Political cartoonists of the day had great fun melding Linderman's two major interests into one.

Yet Linderman's role in the state legislature gave him the chance to do something tangible for the native people. Old Indian acquaintances from earlier years began to drop around to his office, seeking minor favors, such as letters of introduction or references. Because of his interest Linderman took pains to discover how they were faring. In particular he looked up Little Bear and his gypsy band of Crees and Chippewas, some of whom had fled from Canada after the Riel rebellion of 1885. Since that time they had wandered from place to place, seeking a reservation but being shunned as "alien" Indians.

What Linderman found appalled him. The band had moved to the fringes of Helena, where they survived in abject poverty. "Living upon offal garnered from the stingy slaughterhouses on the city's outskirts," he said, "and whatever else they could find in Helena's garbage cans, they were in a state of health that was deplorable."[1] Linderman became their arbiter; he advertised in local newspapers for old clothes and sought funds for food. This launched him on a massive campaign, along with artist Charles M. Russell, *Great Falls Tribune* editor William Bole, and other interested Montanans, to gain a permanent reservation for the homeless wanderers. Finally, in 1916, Linderman learned that the military reserve at Fort Assiniboine, in northeastern Montana, was to be abandoned. At his own expense he traveled to Washington, D.C., where he buttonholed the secretary of the interior and other leading politicians. By the time he left, he had a promise that a portion of the land would become the Rocky Boy's Indian Reservation.

During these years of political activity Linderman frequently met Little Bear, Rocky Boy, Full of Dew, Roasting Stick, and other Cree-Chippewas, who told him numerous legends and stories of Indian life. These later became the subjects of several of his books.

When he left the political arena in 1907, Linderman devoted his energies to the position of state manager for the Germania Life Insurance Company. In his first year he sold more insurance for his company than did any other individual in the United States. For nine years he traveled the state, making plenty of money but rapidly losing contact with his family and friends.

[1]Frank B. Linderman, *Montana Adventure: The Recollections of Frank B. Linderman*, ed. Harold G. Merriam (Lincoln: University of Nebraska Press, 1968), p. 140.

During this period he never gave up his boyhood dreams of Flathead Lake. Now, however, he looked forward to a home there, rather than a trapline. He set an objective of $35,000 in savings, at which time he would give up his business and settle at a favorite spot on Goose Bay. There he planned to devote his full attention to writing.

In 1915, as he neared his goal, he produced his first book, *Indian Why Stories,* published by Charles Scribner's Sons. Illustrated by his friend and compatriot Charles M. Russell, the volume consisted of stories told to him by the Crees, Chippewas, and Blackfeet. Linderman recounted the Indian legends that explained, among other things, why the chipmunk's back is striped, why the mountain lion is long and lean, and why the deer has no gall. "I propose," he said in the introduction, "to tell what I know of these legends, keeping as near as possible to the Indian's style of story-telling."[2]

Two years later Linderman decided to make his move. He sold his insurance business and went to Flathead Lake, building a large log house in the wilderness at the head of Goose Bay. He asked his wife, "I do wonder whether I could make a good living with my pen,"[3] and he was determined to try. Over the next twelve years he wrote seven books: *Indian Lodge-Fire Stories* in 1918; *On a Passing Frontier* and *Indian Old-Man Stories* in 1920; *How It Came About Stories* and a book of verse, *Bunch-Grass and Blue-Joint* in 1921; and *Lige Mounts, Free Trapper* and *Kootenai Why Stories* in 1926. All were published by Scribners.

The books were well received by the public, but by 1922 Linderman was convinced that his publishers were not promoting or selling his books as aggressively as they

[2]Frank B. Linderman, *Indian Why Stories* (New York: Charles Scribners Sons, 1915), p. x.
[3]Linderman, *Montana Adventure,* p. 209.

should. He thought briefly that he might be obliged to go back to the insurance business but then abandoned the idea: "I found long ago that I could not write books and life insurance, and while I am sure that I could earn more money at the latter game I have long ago determined that there are more worthwhile things than dollars."[4] His nest egg of money was gradually declining, however, so in 1924 he bought a hotel in Kalispell and operated it profitably for two years. He also made a brief return to politics, running unsuccessfully for the United States Senate.

During the 1920s, Linderman's writing was often filled with frustration, for while he got consistently good reviews of his books, the sales continued to be discouraging. He knew that he was not writing best sellers, yet the sales appeared to be completely at variance with the popularity of his works.

Then in 1928, the author had an opportunity to visit Crow Chief Plenty Coups at his home in southeastern Montana. He had known the chief for years and now realized that his life story would make a wonderful book. The result was a manuscript that he called simply "American." At that point Linderman concluded that he was unwilling to turn this manuscript over to his old publishers; he was afraid it would be neglected like the others. He made an extended trip to New York, where he arranged to have the John Day Company publish his book in 1930. And the critics raved about *American: The Life Story of a Great Indian, Plenty-coups, Chief of the Crows*. The *New York Times* commented that "nothing altogether comparable . . . has heretofore been added to our literature concerning the American Indian,"[5] while the *Chicago Tribune* praised it as "a clear, unadorned, moving history of a time and a people

---

[4] Ibid., p. 210.
[5] Ibid., p. 211.

both gone."[6] In spite of the Depression, the book went into its third printing within a year.

In the period of elation that followed the lionization of *American*, Linderman turned out several books and manuscripts. Among his works published by John Day Company were *Morning Light* (a reprinting of *Lige Mounts, Free Trapper* under a new title) in 1930; *Old Man Coyote* in 1931; *Red Mother* in 1932; *Stumpy* and the novel *Beyond Law* in 1933. In 1935, on the twenty-fifth anniversary of the establishment of Glacier National Park, the Great Northern Railway published *The Blackfeet Indians* with text by Linderman and illustrations by Weinold Reiss. During this time he also wrote a number of manuscripts that were not published. These included five novels: "Iron Shirt" (1920s); "Chick of Last Chance Gulch" (1936); "Big Jinny" (1927), the story of a grizzly bear; "Henry Plummer" (1922); and "Wolf and the Winds," the work being published here.

By 1933, Linderman's writing career had begun to decline. Although he had changed publishers and was happier with the promotion that was being done on his books, the sales were drastically affected by the Depression. To add to his income, Linderman tried writing for magazines, but his topic, Indians, and his romantic treatment of western lore seemed no longer in fashion. Although he wrote a number of short stories in the 1920s and early 1930s, such as "Dr. and I Stories," "My Kentucky Rifle and Other Rifles," "Fur, Gold, and Grass," and "Poker, Ponies, and a Girl," few were published.

During the 1930s, Linderman avidly pursued a new talent discovered in 1927 when his chance toying with a piece of Joe DeYong's modeling clay produced a bear, lessons in bronze casting at the School of Arts in Santa Barbara,

[6] Ibid.

lifelike models of animals and Indians, and a prolonged effort to capture the image of Charles Russell. At his Flathead Lake home Linderman installed a furnace for bronze-casting his own sculptures. As long as his eyesight permitted, he continued to write and model.

In the hard times in the 1930s, Linderman was one of Montana's favorite sons. He had been awarded an honorary doctorate by Montana State University in 1927, and in later years two schools were named after him. His last public appearance occurred in Santa Barbara, where he had spent the winter of 1937–38 for health reasons. Soon after delivering a lecture there on the Rocky Boy Indians, he died of a heart attack on May 12, 1938.

Over the years Linderman's books have retained their popularity. *Indian Old Man Stories* and *Kootenai Why Stories* were reprinted in 1937; *Indian Why Stories* in 1945 and 1975; *American* in 1962, 1963, and 1972; *Lige Mounts, Free Trapper* in 1964; and *Pretty Shield* in 1972 and 1974. In addition, three of his books were published posthumously: *Recollections of Charley Russell* (Norman: University of Oklahoma Press) in 1963, his autobiography, *Montana Adventure: The Recollections of Frank B. Linderman* (Lincoln: University of Nebraska Press), in 1968; and *Quartzville* (Missoula, Mont.: Mountain Press Publishing Co.), in 1985.

The book now being introduced, *Wolf and the Winds*, was written between October, 1935, and February, 1936, after Linderman returned from his successful venture in New York. Viewing himself as a creative writer, rather than just a transcriber of stories told to him by elderly Indians, he chose to strike out into new literary pastures. Possessing a wealth of information about Indian and Montana history, as well as intimate knowledge of Indian life, he decided to write a fictionalized biography of a Gros Ventre Indian in Montana in the mid-nineteenth century. The story was not published, however, and remained in the Linderman estate until arrangements were made to publish it here for the first time.

To the modern reader Linderman's style may seem dated; yet he wrote with confidence and authority about a subject he knew well. Although the Gros Ventre Indians had not been the primary subjects of his earlier writings, his travels across Montana had included visits to their reservation, and he was personally acquainted with a number of elders of the tribe, as well as the man he calls Wolf.

In the novel Linderman took some broad liberties with the sequence of historical events in Montana. He did so knowingly, believing that the changes were necessary for the unfolding of his fictional tale. For example, in the story he creates a major smallpox epidemic in 1856, when the only two during the century were those in 1837 and 1869. He has the Piegan–Gros Ventre split occurring before the treaty of 1855, when in fact it did not occur until six years after. Similarly, his reasons for the split are at variance with accepted history.

Another liberty, which is probably a reflection of both the 1920s and the author's idealism, is the portrayal of the villain as a half-blood Gros Ventre. This was a common stereotype during the era, one which in part was accepted by those who saw the Indian as a "child of Nature." They perceived the mixed-blood as someone whose influence was evil because the white man's blood coursed through his veins. Linderman, a member of the American Indian Defense Association, likely shared this idealistic view, and he therefore chose that popular stereotype to portray Left Hand.

There can be no question that Linderman knew his field and that the level of accuracy about Indian life in this novel is extremely high. His descriptions of daily life and events are not only correct but extremely sympathetic and understanding for a man writing during an era in which the Indian was either a noble savage or an unfeeling brute. Linderman creates a cast of characters who probably reflect a good cross section of an Indian camp during the days in which his novel is set.

Wolf and the Winds should be seen as a vintage work, with a depth of knowledge and understanding that few authors could ever hope to match.

Wolf and the Winds

by

Frank Bird Linderman

To my nephew
Homer Normann

Foreword

Wolf and the Winds closely follows the life story of an Indian whom I knew. Because his real name is difficult to translate into English, I have called him "Wolf." He lived when there was yet fierce intertribal warfare on these Northern plains, performing most of the deeds which I have ascribed to him; and he died exactly as I have said, an outcast from his people because of his fidelity to his medicine dream and the woman of his choice. Peace to his ashes.

For generations before their migration from the region of Lesser Slave Lake to the Northwestern plains the three tribes of the Blackfeet Nation had been closely associated with the *White-Clay-Men*. Nobody knows when these four tribes of forest people, tiring of the constant warfare waged against them by the powerful Ojibwas, reached their present habitat, nor when they drove the Snakes, and perhaps the Flatheads and Nez Percés, from the plains. Anyhow, soon after the four federated tribes had established themselves as Northern plainsmen the *White-Clay-Men* peacefully detached themselves from the Blackfeet, drifting farther south to the country about the Bighorn Mountains. Here a quarrel between two of their leading chiefs, over the possession of a pair of buffalo kidneys, resulted in a tribal division, one of the disgruntled chieftains leading his followers still farther South (where they became known as *Arapahoes*); the other, retracing his steps, reestablished himself and his band with the Blackfeet (to become *Gros Ventres of the Prairies*).

Most tribal names known to us are purely epithetical, the designations of enemy tribesmen, or early French voyageurs. The *Gros Ventres of the Praries* (French, meaning *Big Bellies*) have continued to call themselves *White-Clay-Men*. They are the same people as the *Arapahoes;* and *Arapaho* (a Crow word, meaning *Tatooed Marks Plenty of*) is itself epithetical.

The long-established peace of the four federated tribes was finally broken by sudden war between the Gros Ventres and the Pecunnies [Pikunis] (a tribe of the Blackfeet Nation), brought about, they now declare, by a cunning trick which had been played upon them by their mutual enemies the Flatheads. The exact date of the beginning of this warfare is difficult to set. However, it was soon *after* the Stevens Treaty of 1855, and *not immediately prior* to this treaty, as I have arbitrarily placed it for story purposes.

The average oldtimer in the Northwest who too often judged the Indian wholly by his depredations may easily believe that I have idealized him. If I have, then it is idealization by omission, by leaving unstressed the traits of his character which have been well known for hundreds of years, so well known that with these traits alone the Indian's place among humankind seemed to me to have been forever fixed. I have known the red man of the Northwest for half a century. He is not a saint. On the contrary, he has many times qualified as a nearly perfect devil, and here I do not defend him further than to declare that for every atrocity perpetrated by him against the white race I will undertake to name two equally revolting crimes which have been committed against him by white men.

F. B. L.

BOOK ONE

Chapter 1

On an early fall day about the year 1835, a village of Prairie
Gros Ventres was pitched on the wide plains near the
mouth of Milk River on the upper Missouri. Here a son
was born to Horned-bull and Small-voice, his woman,
Gros Ventres of no great importance. The village moved
twenty miles on the following day. With it went the family
of Horned-bull, without inconvenience or objection. The
tribe was on its fall hunt for buffalo, tenaciously following
the immense herds until all the travois* were heavily laden
with dried meat, and even the cavernous bellies of the village dogs were filled. Racks of red buffalo meat, drying in
the bright sunlight, had stretched from one end of the village to the other in every camp it had made. As fast as it
had dried sufficiently to ensure its keeping until further
care could be given it the meat had been removed from the
racks, and more, fresh from the plains, had taken its place
until the women had declared that there was enough.
Then the Gros Ventres turned back up the Missouri, going
into their winter quarters, plentifully supplied with food
until summer came again. The women had been too busy
until now; but now they came to see the young son of

*From the *French Voyageur.*—F. B. L.

Horned-bull and Small-voice, his woman. Swathed in his back cradle that leaned against a bale of buffalo robes, the baby watched them come and go with the same vacant stare out of his black eyes. The women admired him, or pretended they did. His mother, Small-voice, adored him. "See his eyes! Note how bright they are," she would say, pridefully. "His grandfather has named him *Wolf*." And sometimes she would add, "My son will be a brave warrior. I have dreamed."

"Of course, if she has dreamed, her son may distinguish himself," the women agreed. "But the child is small. Besides, Small-voice may have been mistaken in the interpretation of her dream. It may not have been a medicine dream at all," they said, gossiping. However, time would tell about the son of Small-voice. But the day of its telling was far off. Meantime the child was small, "nothing to be making talk of coming greatness," the women said.

When Wolf was three years old a brother occupied his old place in the back cradle. But the eyes of the new baby were not like Wolf's. His mother did not speak to her visitors of dreams concerning him. He was christened "Rain"; and from the day that his mother put Rain into the back cradle Wolf would have given his life for his brother. He would sit for hours looking fondly into the baby's eyes. He sang for him, danced for him, as though his very life depended upon Rain's happiness. Even after he had reached his fourth year and could ride a horse when the village moved, Wolf rode behind his mother so that he might watch his brother on his mother's back. His affection for Rain became the talk of the village. "Wolf is more like a girl than a boy," the young women said.

"Ahh, you do not understand," smiled the older women. "Do you not see that among the four-year-olds Wolf is the leader, the mischief-maker, that his little arrows go straighter than those of his companions, that he runs faster than they do? When something that torments you has been done by the little boys, catch Wolf. Ask him who did it. If he, himself, is guilty, he will tell you. If he is not guilty, he will say so. Then ask him if he knows who did the thing that tormented you. Nearly always he will say 'Yes.' But try to make him name the guilty boy. He will not answer. You will never make him tell you. And yet Wolf will not lie. Looking straight into your eyes he will defy you with his silence. Wolf is different from most of the other boys. Remember that his mother, Small-voice, dreamed before Wolf was born. Yes, he is different. However, a man may love his brother, and yet be a man. Someday you will see."

Often when his brother had grown a little older, Wolf carried Rain with him on his horse when the village moved; and it was always moving since the tribes followed the great herds of buffalo for meat. Even when the warriors began to notice him, to commend his skill with the bow and arrow, to tell him tales of war, that ecstatical period that lifted Indian boys into the wind-blown clouds of ambition, Wolf continued to give adoring attention to Rain. Respectfully listening to the advice of renowned warriors, untiring at all games which would strengthen his muscles, train his eyes, give him the power of endurance, Wolf spent part of each day training Rain. In this he was an exacting master, quick to praise accomplishment and slow to condemn failure.

So proficient was Wolf in his teaching that when he was ten years old many boys joined his classes. He grew a little arrogant, at times assuming in the presence of his youthful companions the manners of a seasoned warrior; and yet his self-reliance and tenacity of purpose to attain perfection in all trials of skill and endurance commanded the respect of everybody. Copying their energetic leader, who worked tirelessly to maintain his supremacy, the boys were often difficult to manage, which worried their mothers.

When, in his twelfth year, Wolf organized his followers into a secret society which he called *The Badgers,* the women were openly hostile toward him, particularly after *The Badgers* had twice mysteriously disappeared from the village, both times remaining away overnight. There was always danger from Sioux or Crow war parties; and *The Badgers* were mere boys, the oldest among them not yet thirteen years of age. And yet most of the old warriors, themselves honorable members of societies within the tribe, winked at Wolf's doings, covertly smiling at the anxiety of their women. Even when *The Badgers,* led by Wolf, stole twenty-six Gros Ventre horses, spiriting the animals away to their camp up the Missouri River, the men found no fault. On the contrary, forgetting the village's quick consternation at the discovery of the loss of the horses, the warriors, all of them excepting the horse guards themselves, commended Wolf and *The Badgers,* because their feat had been performed while the horses had been under guard in broad daylight. "Ah, Wolf is clever," they chuckled over their pipes. "Someday he will be a chief," they said.

But the women were determined to break up Wolf's society; and because corporal punishment was never practiced by the plains Indians, they resorted to ridicule. Led by old Duck-woman, the village scold, a widow having no children of her own, thirty mothers invaded a meeting of *The Badgers,* seating themselves among their astonished sons, their manner that of women visiting a gathering of girls. Taking over the meeting as though it were their own and all present were females, they opened a discussion on the proper care of newly born babies, the outraged *Badgers* bolting for the door of their flimsy brush lodge.

Grateful because his mother had not joined in this insult to *The Badgers,* Wolf immediately determined upon reprisal, presenting to his followers a plan to particularly torment Duck-woman, whom he had always disliked. Waiting for a dark night, the boys roped, threw, and hogtied the wildest half-grown colt in all the Gros Ventre horse herd, carrying him bodily to Duck-woman's lodge. Then, after satisfying themselves that the old woman was asleep, the young ruffians silently pulled the ground pegs, cautiously lifted the lodge skin, cut the colt's lashings, and pushed him inside the lodge, dropping the lodge skin behind him.

Instantly the woman's screaming roused the sleeping village; but before help could come the crazed colt, wild as a buffalo bull, plunging, striking, and kicking in the dark interior, had killed Duck-woman.

The Badgers never held another meeting. Wolf, readily assuming full responsibility for Duck-woman's death, lost his arrogance, for a time seeming to shun his former companions for Rain's company alone. Never talkative, he was even more silent now, his wonderful eyes clouded by baffling mental disturbance. Blackening his face, in mourning, as though Duck-woman had been closely related to him by blood, the boy sat alone for hours on high knoll tops staring fixedly at the wide horizon as though struggling with his inner self. His wise mother, understanding her son's travail, was especially careful of him now, never by even a glance criticizing his conduct.

In the spring of his fifteenth year Wolf, who was yet thin in body, had grown tall, the sharpness of his eyes seeming to emphasize his spareness so much that he appeared frail. "The time has come when I should try to dream," he told his father one day when the Gros Ventre village had been pitched at the foot of the Bear Paw mountains.

"There is yet time, my son, plenty of time," counseled Horned-bull, remembering the fatigue and torture attending his own medicine dream. "You had better wait another year," he advised.

Wolf said no more. But the next morning when Small-voice kindled her fire in the lodge Wolf's bedrobe was vacant. "Where is your brother?" she asked Rain, lifting the lodge door to look out at the rapidly unfolding leaves and flowers.

"Wolf has gone into the high mountains to try to dream," anwered Rain, solemnly; and then, for a moment only the new fire made sounds in the lodge of Horned-bull.

The mother, sighing heavily, placed dry sticks upon the fire. "Oh, have pity on him, all of you *Who Live Without Fire*,"* she whispered, her heart heavy with thoughts of her son's coming ordeal.

"Ho! Lift up your heart, Woman; let it sing, now that your son has gone to dream," said Horned-bull. And chanting his own medicine song the father of Wolf danced in his lodge. Then, kneeling, he lighted his red-stone pipe, offering its stem first to the Sun, the Father, and then to the Earth, the Mother of all things on the world. Lifting his eyes to the bit of sky that showed through the smoke hole these impassioned words went up to the supernatural ones. "My son is out there! My son is out there in the high mountains! Oh, let him dream. Let him dream a great dream. Send him Helpers, some of you *Who Live Without Fire*. Send him good Helpers, so that he may become a great warrior, be a chief among his people. Oh, hear me, one who has dreamed. Send my son good Helpers!"

"Ho, Woman," he said, suddenly ending his appeal, "let your heart sing. Our son will dream a great dream."

*Supernatural ones, Spirits of the dead, etc.—F. B. L.

But the heart of Small-voice would not be lifted. Anxiety, pity, and perhaps even pride had pressed it to the ground. The day of her own dream's fulfillment was at hand. She knew that her son would dream a great dream, that he would become a renowned warrior. In all this there was cause for pride. Small-voice felt this pride; but stabbing her heart like a sharp thorn was the fear that Wolf's life would be moulded by his dream, the dream which she, herself, had dreamed that he would dream.

Chapter 2

The first sign of morning found Wolf far from the village. In his eagerness to feel fatigue, walking rapidly, often running, he had reached the base of a high mountain before sunrise. Now his body must be prepared for the desired dream. As though he had always known the exact spot to be chosen for this preparation, Wolf stopped beside a creek that dashed white water against a ledge of jagged rock, dropped his robe, hastily cut sixteen slender willows from a thicket that grew on a tiny meadow opposite the white water. At his feet, washing the meadow's bank, reaching even to its rank grass, the water eddied in a deep pool, icy, and clear as the air. "Ah," he whispered, seeing the perfection of choice that was here. "They have led me to this place." Feverishly now the boy sharpened both ends of his gathered willows and bending the slender withes thrust their sharpened ends into the soft ground so that they made a frame shaped like an inverted bowl, large enough to permit him to lie in a curled position within, tying the willows with bark at their intersections. This frame he covered with his buffalo robe, stopping all openings with his leggings and clout, banking the bottom all round with leaves and dirt. While a fire which he had kindled nearby heated small boulders, Wolf raised the

14

edge of the robe covering nearest the fire and with his knife and hands scooped out a small pit inside the sweatlodge, near its center; and into this pit he rolled the nearly white-hot stones.

Going to the creek, he filled a buffalo-horn ladle with water, carefully placing it inside the sweat lodge. Now he removed his moccasins and, straightening his naked body, lifted his eyes to the blue sky, his lips moving rapidly, passionately, in a supplication to the supernatural: "Oh, *You Who Live Without Fire* pity me. Let me dream! Give me knowledge, a Helper, so that I may be of service to my people."

Four times, each growing in intensity, he repeated his appeal, his words fanatical, breathless, the fine muscles of his boyish body straining against themselves until, with a sudden glad cry, he thrust his arms upward, holding them rigidly toward a soaring Golden Eagle, a *war eagle*, its wide wings motionless in the bright sunlight. "Oh, Eagle, Great One, you have come to help me," he called, his voice shaking with gratitude.

Thrilled by this good omen which had set his blood leaping with happiness, Wolf crept into his sweat lodge, sprinkling water from the horn ladle upon the hot stones. Rising steam instantly enveloped him. Perspiration poured from his body. Again and again he sprinkled the stones with water, lying curled upon the ground, his muscles relaxing in the enervating steam until he felt weakness creeping over his limbs. His heart began to pound noisily, his head seeming to swim. And yet once more Wolf sprinkled the hot stones, gasping for breath as he groped in the blinding steam to find a safe resting place for the horn ladle. Once, in desperation, his hand sought blindly to lift the lodge covering for breath; but the tenacity of his will restrained it. He could hear perspiration dripping from his body, hear his heart protesting against its stifling confinement, when at last he burst from the sweat lodge and plunged headlong into the icy pool of the creek.

A flash, a few sharp strokes, and the boy's head appeared above the eddying water. Reaching the shore he sat for a moment to rest, his breath coming in short gasps. Then, weakened, and yet happily conscious of a stinging exhilaration that crept over his body, he arose, picked up a small buckskin pouch near the sweat lodge, and, naked, began climbing the mountain to try to dream. Unmindful of obstacles, with no thought of saving, but rather to prodigally spend, himself, Wolf set his course toward the highest peak, frantically clambering across slides of sharp shale which wounded his feet, and up nearly sheer cliffs that bruised his knees and finger tips. Gaining the summit where deep drifts of snow defied the suns of June, Wolf, as though mysteriously guided, walked straight to the flat, smooth rock on the edge of a cliff so dizzying in its sheer pitch downward to the tumbled rocks beneath that when he dared to look down a quick stab of fear drove him backward. Catching his breath, he whispered thanks to the mysterious power which had benevolently led him so directly to this terrifying spot; and then he hastened to find *ground cedar,* a kind of yew, for a bed near the edge of the cliff.

Scarcely a breeze stirred on the mountaintop. The light on the snowbanks on both sides of the rocky summit was blinding, the sun's heat upon his naked body intense, as he tore from the ground the desired sweet-smelling, prickly boughs for his dream bed. Carrying them to the cliff, he spread them upon the smooth rock, arranging them hurriedly, carelessly, since they were intended to torture, and not to comfort, him when he had found exhaustion of mind and body. Now, to remove all odor of mankind from his person, Wolf took sweet sage from his buckskin pouch; and after offering the fragrant leaves to the North, East, South and West, he applied them to his body, rubbing vigorously.

He had not rested a moment since leaving the village. Now, tossing his buckskin pouch onto his bed, he set out, running along the narrow, rocky mountaintop, calling for Helpers. His feet were bruised and swollen; the rocks were stained with their blood. Darkness came and a night wind from the North. Sharp cold mercifully benumbed his lacerated feet, and yet Wolf, piteously calling for Helpers, drove his weary legs on and on until, after midnight, he stumbled over a jagged rock, dangerously cutting his thigh.

The fall partially stunned him, so that for moments he lay as though asleep. Staggering to his feet, he felt his hot blood gushing from the wound in his thigh. "I shall soon grow weak now," he whispered, gratefully, running again, his constant calling for Helpers unanswered. He remembered the first signs of morning, the dying of the night, the sun's rising, the subsiding of the cold nightwind; but how or when he found his bed on the edge of the dizzying cliff he never knew. "*They* must have led me," he said afterwards.

It may have been the following night, though Wolf never knew exactly when his dream began or ended, since it was not until the afternoon of the fourth day that his father found him, unconscious, on the mountainside far below his dream bed. Anyhow, the boy was in darkness when he heard his name pronounced, "Wolf!"

"Yes," he answered, stirring in his dream.

"Wolf! Wolf!" came the voice again, this time near his feet.

17

"Yes, yes, I am here. I am Wolf," he whispered, wondering if they heard. "Where are you?" he asked, louder, his voice sounding hollow and far away.

"We are here. We are the Winds. We have brought you a Helper."

Sitting up, Wolf saw a white, transparent form at his feet, at the very edge of the awful cliff. Slowly, as though a film were clearing from his eyes, the outline of the pale figure grew distinct. The Eagle, the war eagle, whitened now by the supernatural ones, was there; the same Eagle that he had seen soaring above his sweat lodge! And yet the Eagle seemed to be only a feathery form, white as snow, light as the air.

"Wolf," said The Winds, "we have work to do. We are going away now to begin the work of teaching you a great lesson if you are willing to learn. While we are gone, while we are working for you, listen to the words of the *One* who is sitting at your feet. Ho!"

And then, with a sudden swirl that ruffled the Eagle's feathers as though nothing held them together, The Winds were gone. So still was the world just there that Wolf could hear his heart beating like a war drum. In this silence the white bird turned his back to the dreamer, his sharp talons gripping the cliff's edge. Wolf could see the night stars shining through the Eagle's body; and when the Eagle moved a little slab of shale fell from the cliff's face, shattering noisily on the rocks below. Wolf, shuddering, heard the fragments scatter far down where the night was darker; and yet no sign, no word, came from the Winds. A bright star fell, shooting across the sky, leaving a short trail of light behind it; and then Wolf felt a faint breeze on his face.

"I hear them coming. Your Helpers are coming," said the Eagle, his voice sounding afraid. "Come, sit beside me, my son," he whispered, moving sidewise a little. "Let your feet hang over the cliff."

Afraid, and yet not daring to show his fear of the chasm beyond the cliff's edge, Wolf crept beside the white Eagle, letting his feet hang over the smooth rock that felt icy cold beneath his naked knees. A quick gust of wind brushed his forehead, moving his hair. Not daring to look down, he fixed his eyes on the dark emptiness ahead, upon the endless plains.

Suddenly, where the starry sky met the far-off edge of the grasslands, a bright light lifted itself high, growing wider and more and more brilliant as it moved westward, toward them on the cliff. Vivid colors, even more gorgeous than those of the rainbow, shot like thin, fiery arrows across the yellow light of the fiery cloud. It was sweeping toward the cliff, coming rapidly, like a dangerous storm. The sharp arrows of green, blue, red and black that darted downward through the yellow fire made hissing sounds as hot stones do when water is poured upon them; and now The Winds blew fiercely, bending Wolf backward until he cried out in terror.

"Be not afraid, my Son. Look carefully at this thing which The Winds are showing you," warned the Eagle. "If you learn the lesson that is here, you may save your people," he added, cryptically.

Forcing his body erect against the fierce Winds that lashed his unbraided hair, Wolf seized the cliff's edge with his hands. The cloud of fire was upon him, scorching his shoulders. He was conscious of an odor that nauseated him; and then the apparition was gone!

As though suddenly relieved of a great burden, Wolf drew up his feet. "Wait! There is yet more to see. Look again to the East, my Son," admonished the Eagle.

A soft, white light illumined all the plains now. Wolf could even see the grass there, and the sage, the courses of the rivers, and many wolves. Far away toward the North and West there were tribes, enemies of his people, their lodges pitched in pretty places. But from East to West along the course which the beautiful, fiery cloud had taken, there was nothing, not even a lone buffalo. It was as though the way of the cloud had been swept clean of all life.

"For some reason they have moved. The buffalo have wandered away from our country, from all the country over which the beautiful cloud passed; and the tribes have followed the buffalo. Both will return," thought Wolf, strangely troubled.

"No, my Son," said Eagle, knowing the boy's thoughts. "No. The buffalo are dead. They will never return."

As the Eagle spoke, The Winds came to Wolf from the East. The nauseating odor grew stronger, so strong that Wolf sickened. Covering his face with his hands, he heard the rapid firing of guns, loud and terrifying. The firing seemed to be on all sides of him; and then suddenly it ceased. The Winds were gone again.

"Look once more to the East, my Son," urged the Eagle. "Can you see? Do you see your plains now?" he asked, moving nearer the boy.

Skeletons of buffalo whitened the way the fiery cloud had traversed. As far as Wolf could see, the bleaching bones seemed to reach from East to West over the wide grasslands, to the foot of the mountain where he had made his dream bed. There was no living tribesman in sight, not even an enemy.

"This is all. The Winds have finished. Do you understand what they would have you know, my Son?" said the Eagle.

"No," answered Wolf, his heart heavy with fear.

"Listen then; and when you have listened, think deeply of what your Helpers, The Winds, have shown you. I am speaking for *them*, your Helpers," said the Eagle. "The beautiful, fiery cloud is the white man. The brilliant arrows are his cunning ways, his trade goods, his bright blankets, which so easily attract your people. The sweep of the beautiful cloud represents the white man's coming, the course he will travel across the plains. He will sweep them clean, leave nothing that lives. Desolation, want, and death will follow him. In his dealings with your people he will cheat and rob them as he always has cheated and robbed the other tribes. His tongue is forked; and he dares to mock his God. I have spoken, my Son. I, too, will be your Helper if you walk straight and are not afraid."

Then, as though the air had taken him away, the Eagle was gone. Wolf, drawing up his legs, heard another slab of shale fall from the cliff's face, shattering into fragments among the jagged rocks below.

Chapter 3

Wolf did not know when he left his dream bed. His consciousness was aroused by the voices of his father and brother, who had carried him from the mountainside to his sweat lodge, there reviving him with cold water. And yet, even when consciousness had returned to him, Wolf did not speak to Horned-bull or his brother, Rain. He must first enter the sweat lodge before conversing with mankind. Lying upon a buffalo robe where they had placed him, he silently watched his father and brother prepare the sweat lodge, heat the stones, and bring the ladle of water from the creek. Then, creeping, he curled his gaunt body around the hot stones, letting Horned-bull himself sprinkle them with water and close the opening. No hand might properly touch Wolf until he had entered the water after his cleaning sweat bath so that, unaided, he must walk to the creek. Horned-bull, knowing that the boy was already dangerously weak, did not wait long before lifting the lodge covering, bidding his son to come out. But once he was in the water, his father's willing hands helped Wolf out again, finishing the ordeal.

Late in the afternoon they reached the village, Rain, afoot, leading the travois horse bearing Wolf, and Horned-bull walking behind. Pride shone on the faces of both the father and the brother. Both were singing when they entered the village. Their coming caused men and women to gather, to follow the travois to the lodge of Horned-bull, where Small-voice, Wolf's anxious mother, was waiting to receive her son.

Upon entering the lodge with his mother, Wolf heard Horned-bull speaking to a chief outside. The weary boy had scarcely seated himself when a crier, riding about the village, began calling, "Ho! Wolf, the son of Horned-bull has suffered, has dreamed a medicine dream. In the morning he will relate his dream in the lodge of the Wise-ones, so that we, his people, may know its meaning. Go, all you young men. Follow the example of Wolf, the son of Horned-bull. Try to dream. Your people need many Helpers. Ho!"

Fondly smiling at the soberness of Rain, who could not keep his eyes from staring at his brother's bandaged thigh, Wolf listened to the crier's message, saw the pride that shown in his mother's eyes, heard the low voices of men and women talking outside, as though important news had reached the village, watched his father fill and light his red-stone pipe, offering its stem to the *Mysterious Ones*, as though yet in his dream. But when his father, after taking three deep draughts from the pipe, passed it to him, Wolf's heart warmed with pride of accomplishment. He had dreamed.

But the thrill which this thought gave him did not last. Fear came to him, fear that the Wise-ones might not believe in his dream, that they might smile at his credulity, as he had seen them smile. This would crush him. "Mine may not have a medicine dream," he said sadly, his eyes dazed.

"Yes, yes. Yours *was* a great dream, a medicine dream." There was challenge in his mother's words. Rising from her place in the lodge, she knelt beside Wolf. "I *know!* Oh, I know, my Son. I have long known that you would have this dream, and that if you follow it, as you will, you will suffer," she said, covering her face with her hands.

"Lift up your heart, Woman. Our son has dreamed, has found a Helper of whom he has not yet spoken," said Horned-bull, his voice a little stern.

"Ah, a Helper! Yes, if our people will listen. But they will not listen. I know. Oh, I know," sighed Small-voice, going hastily to the lodge door that had been lifted, a bright face peering bashfully within.

"Oh, Breath-feather,[1] you are welcome. Come sit beside me," said Small-voice, spreading a buffalo robe for the young daughter of Red-moccasin, the tribe's war chief.

"I have brought sweet grass," said the girl, embarrassed now that she had come to the lodge. "May I put it upon your fire?" she asked, avoiding Wolf's eyes, her cheeks flushing.

"Yes, Breath-feather," Horned-bull answered proudly, raking four living coals from the lodge fire to receive the sacred offering, his eyes watching his son.

The slender girl, nearly as tall as Wolf, her long braids of black hair reaching to her waist, laid the sweet grass upon the coals; and then, softly as a shadow, she returned to her seat to watch the white smoke of the burning grass curl upward, filling the lodge of Horned-bull and Small-voice with fragrance. When her eyes dropped again, they met Wolf's in a swift passing that gave them nothing. Reverently she bowed her head while Horned-bull chanted a prayer to the *Mysterious Ones.*

The chanting ended. Small-voice showed the girl a pair of leggings which she was making, the two women

---

[1] A downy feather.—F. B. L.

talking softly of needlework while Horned-bull filled and lighted his pipe, formally passing it to his son, as to an acknowledged warrior. As he accepted the pipe, Wolf's eyes met Breath-feather's, lingering until the girl's lowered in embarrassment.

"I have work that I must finish," she said softly to Small-voice, rising and lifting the door.

When she was gone, Small-voice folded the guest robe, her eyes smiling happily. "Breath-feather is a pretty girl, a good worker," she said, her back to Wolf.

Horned-bull put the pipe into its pouch. The girl was the daughter of Red-moccasin; and this war chief was a proud man, a man who had counted many coups.[2] Have you been courting so soon?" he asked teasingly, feeling proud of his son, nevertheless.

"No," Wolf answered, shortly. "I must first go to war, count coup, before thinking of women. I have not yet even talked to women."

"Wolf saved Breath-feather's life," Rain blurted, avoiding his brother's eyes.

"When?" Small-voice straightened to look at her oldest son.

"Last summer when she was swimming," answered Rain doggedly. "I saw it all. Breath-feather would have died if Wolf had not saved her. She was nearly dead when he carried her from the river."

"Does her mother know this?" asked Small-voice.

"No. Nobody knows. Breath-feather was swimming alone when the thing happened. Because she feared her

[2] From the *French Voyageur*. The rules governing the counting of coups differed somewhat among the tribes of the plains; but with all of them striking an armed enemy with the hand, or with something held in the hand, before killing him, or permitting him to escape unhurt, counted the most honorable of coups.—F. B. L.

mother would not let her go swimming again she asked us not to tell. But if Wolf——"

"And now you have *told*," Wolf interrupted, reproach in his eyes.

Rain hung his head, the index finger of one hand digging at the ground. He would have given anything if he could have recalled his words. They had been forced from him by his pride for his brother; now he had told the secret, had broken faith with Wolf.

"It is as though you had not spoken, my Son," Smallvoice said understandingly, her hand on Rain's shoulder. "Your father's ears have heard nothing of this, nor have mine. Forgive your brother, Wolf," she said, turning. "It was his heart that spoke."

"It was nothing," laughed Wolf. "I have already forgotten it, so there is nothing to forgive." Then, to his father, "Will Red-moccasin be in the lodge with the Wise-ones?" he asked, thinking doubtfully of the morrow.

"Yes, of course," Horned-bull answered seriously.

"And Black-tongue?" the boy inquired.

"Yes," said his father again. "Black-tongue will be there."

It was Black-tongue whom Wolf most dreaded. Old and stern, wisest of all, Black-tongue was a veritable hierarchy in himself, especially to the boys of the tribe, who had themselves built up stories of his mysterious power. That Black-tongue had once walked on water was a tribal belief; and it was whispered that he had once "looked an enemy to death." He seemed always to frown upon frivolous youth. Now, thinking of Black-tongue, Wolf dreaded the ordeal in the medicine lodge.

"It is in the lodge of Black-tongue that you are to tell your dream," said Horned-bull. "Black-tongue is wise. His heart is good. I once saw him heal a badly wounded man by touching him with his hand; and there was nothing in his hand."

"Oh, have no fear of Black-tongue, Wolf, my son," Small-voice said, earnestly, knowing what was passing in the boy's mind. "You have dreamed. In the medicine lodge you will not lie. You will speak wih a straight tongue. This is all that will be expected of you. Have no fear. And now sleep, my Son, that your mind may be like a sharp knife when the sun rises."

But for a long time after the lodge of Horned-bull was quiet Wolf did not sleep. The scarred face and searching eyes of old Black-tongue would not be banished. Turning uneasily on his robe, ever so quietly that he might not disturb his mother, who he knew was as deeply concerned for the morrow as himself, Wolf thought a hundred times before he slept, "If Black-tongue smiles at me in the medicine lodge, I shall die of shame."

Chapter 4

The village crier, summoning the Wise-ones[1] to the lodge of Black-tongue, awakened Wolf, who had slept late. Taking only a drink of cold water, the boy followed his father out of the lodge, his hair, unbraided and loose since first entering the sweat lodge at the foot of the mountain, ruffling in the morning breeze.

The lodge of Black-tongue was pitched at the far end of the village of more than two hundred lodges that seemed, somehow, to challenge Wolf. As though yet in his dream he smelled the smoke of scores of new fires, heard horses whinny, felt the eyes of his companions, and those of women and girls, peering at him from lifted lodge doors as he passed. But when he neared the well-known lodge of the old medicine man, with its mysterious paintings upon it, he was suddenly conscious that The Winds were behind him, that they were going with him to meet the Wise ones. "Oh, Winds, I thank you," he whispered, deeply grateful. Strengthened now, he was no longer afraid when his father lifted the door of the painted lodge.

Twelve men were there, eleven besides Black-tongue, who sat at the head of the lodge, not only because the

[1]Medicine men.—F. B. L.

lodge was his own but because of his eminence among the wise ones of the tribe. On the ground before him, facing the door where Wolf knelt, there was the bleached skull of a buffalo bull bearing red hieroglyphics of which the boy knew nothing. Beyond this, toward Wolf, there were four huge claws of a grizzly bear; and in the center of the lodge where coals of fire smoldered, sweet grass was burning. Black-tongue, rising to his knees, invoked aid from the *Mysterious Powers*, his scarred face strangely softened. Then, sitting back upon his heels, "Speak, Wolf, son of Horned-bull," he said, simply, looking into the boy's eyes.

Wolf could feel the tense eagerness that seized these strong men when for the first time since entering the lodge he swept their faces with a quick glance. Speaking only to Black-tongue, whom he had somehow and suddenly come to look upon as his friend, Wolf related his dream, his eyes never wavering. "I have finished," he said, finally, without offering the white Eagle's interpretation of his dream.

Black-tongue, rising, with solemn dignity took Wolf by the hand, seating him at the left of the head of the lodge, the place of honor. "Yours was a great dream, my Son," he said, filling the ceremonial pipe for passing. When the pipe had returned to his hands, Black-tongue, using nearly the white Eagle's words, interpreted Wolf's dream. "The meaning is clear," he told the others in the lodge. "The *Powerful Ones* have warned us that we must have nothing to do with white men, that the white man's coming to our country means the end of the buffalo, the end of life for us. From this day onward I will not trade with white men, will not own goods they make, nor use their weapons. I have spoken."

"But our enemies are armed with the guns that white men make. We cannot be strong against our enemies unless we have guns," Red-moccasin, the war chief, pointed out.

Two others concurred in this. "Let us trade only for guns and powder and lead," they urged, feeling that otherwise Wolf's dream was truly a warning.

For answer Black-tongue drew a red blanket from his shoulders, throwing it out of the lodge. "I have finished with white men," he said, sternly. "I will go no more to their forts to trade. But I will at any time go to them to fight, as our father's fought, with our bows and arrows. Dare you laugh at this warning?" he asked, scanning every man's face in the silence that followed.

"Your medicine is the Wind, Wolf," said Black-tongue, as though the boy and himself were alone in the lodge. "The war eagle, and The Winds, a strong medicine, my Son," he added, half to himself.

Even in his elation, in which he felt himself drawn closely to Black-tongue, Wolf sensed the dissatisfaction which the interpretation of his dream had engendered among the Wise-ones in the medicine lodge. He knew that his dream had divided these powerful men and that the influence of each would be far-reaching among the clans of the tribe. He also knew that there would be portentous discussion of his dream now; and possessing the white Eagle's interpretation, he did not wish to hear it. "We will go," he said softly to his father, when Black-tongue began again to fill the ceremonial pipe. Before the pipe was lighted for passing, Wolf and his father left the lodge.

When the door fell behind him, Wolf believed that he had stepped from boyhood to maturity. He felt strangely alone, as though his dream had separated him from his people. And yet he felt no resentment. Instead, he believed that The Winds and the other *Mysterious Ones* had honored him above all his tribesmen, that they had chosen him, a boy, to keep the feet of his people in the way of their fathers. That he might fail did not enter his mind. His firm faith in The Winds, and the war eagle, his Helpers, precluded all thoughts of failure. Not once did he consider the discomfort, or ostracism, that might come to himself through his constancy of purpose.

"We have visitors." His father's words were filled with interest. A woman of middle age, wearing scarlet head silk, was getting down from her horse beside the door of Horned-bull's lodge. Even before she had called out or lifted the door, Wolf's mother came out of the lodge, warmly greeting the women.

"Your sister has come," she called to Horned-bull, who quickened his steps, his eyes suddenly happy.

Wolf, after greeting his aunt, Running-deer, whom he had not seen for more than ten years, turned to speak words of welcome to a boy of his own age, a cousin who was yet mounted and holding the lead rope of a pack horse. "Get down, Left-hand, my cousin," he said, cheerily. "I will help you unpack your horse."

But the women, talking and laughing excitedly, insisted upon unpacking the horse themselves, carrying the packs into Horned-bull's lodge, Wolf, Rain and Left-hand seating themselves inside with Horned-bull, who was graciousness itself. Wolf's keen eyes were instantly busy in their appraisal of Left-hand, whom he had not seen since both were toddlers. There was an evident air of superiority about his cousin. Taller than Wolf, and heavier, Left-hand was handsome despite several scarcely perceptible pits left upon his chin and forehead by smallpox. His dark eyes were restless, shifty and deeply set, his thin-lipped mouth petulant and a little weak. And yet withal the half-breed, a veritable dandy, vain as a strutting sage cock, was strikingly attractive, even though his perfumed braids of long brown hair, wound with green silk, his red shirt, and beaded moccasins were an abomination to Wolf, who had never seen the young man's father, a white man who had been banished from white society. Now he listened while his cousin, answering Horned-bull's questions, told in a few sentences the story of their abandonment and his mother's enforced return to her people, the Gros Ventres. The white father of Left-hand had lived with Running-deer for fifteen years far down the Missouri River. Now this white man had "gone away," had been gone for two years. Lately a letter, containing a little money for Running-deer, had come to another trader from the big river. Left-hand's father was not coming back to the plains. "My father is rich now. He will stay with his own people," the boy ended with admiration, if not real pride in his voice.

"You are welcome here with us," said Horned-bull simply. "You shall have a good lodge of your own, and I will kill your meat until you have learned to use a strong bow."

Small-voice, knowing that the travelers would be hungry, had put a kettle of buffalo meat on the lodge fire as soon as they arrived. Now she placed the meat before them, the family of Horned-bull watching them eat alone as Indian hosts do. There was much to talk about, much to tell. And yet there were no tears, no outward show of grief, no tales of hardship from Running-deer, who showed not the least resentment against her former lord, who had so heartlessly left her and her son to shift for themselves. Life for these people of the vast northwestern plains had always been uncertain and hard. Whatever *was* to be *would* be. There was no good in complaining or in finding fault with fate.

Anyhow, besides life and the day itself, Running-deer felt that she had been generously compensated for her abandonment. "See my pretty things," she laughed, merrily unpacking and untying bundles to display several bright-colored calico gowns, two scarlet blankets, and a half-dozen silk handkerchiefs of varied hues.

"And these are Left-hand's," she proudly explained, spreading four new shirts for the admiration of her relations. Made by herself, the handiwork perfect, the garments were tawdry, ranging in color from bright red to green. "This pretty one is a little small for you, my Son," she said, holding up the green shirt. "Will you give it to Wolf, your cousin?" she asked as though uncertain of the boy's generosity.

Flashing a glance at Left-hand, Wolf saw sullen greed in his cousin's eyes. "I do not want the shirt," he said, shortly, remembering his dream.

As though he had heard neither his mother's question nor Wolf's declaration, Left-hand drew from a buckskin pouch at his belt a short-stemmed white man's pipe, a new jackknife, and tobacco, the display of property giving him pleasure. Cutting the tobacco, the half-breed filled and lighted his pipe, smoking alone as though Horned-bull and his cousins were not present.

Stung by her son's rudeness and silence, Running-deer hastily drew a ring from her finger. "I give you this," she said, offering the brass band to Small-voice.

"No, no. Keep your ring. I cannot wear a ring. A ring would hurt my finger when I work," smiled Small-voice. And then, because to refuse a gift is to insult the giver, she added: "Running-deer, Wolf, my son, has dreamed. I cannot wear the white man's things. It is forbidden me. But you are not Wolf's mother. Put the ring back on your finger," she said tolerantly.

Wolf's wondering eyes met his mother's. He had not yet spoken of his dream to his mother.

Chapter 5

In spite of Red-moccasin, the other prominent leaders, Black-tongue's counsel prevailed, so that Wolf's dream nearly brought on a tribal declaration of war against white men. For more than three years the Gros Ventres did not visit the trading posts, carefully avoiding the use of white men's goods. This forbearance caused little grumbling even among the younger men, most of them looking upon Wolf as their leader. But when in the fourth year after the warning dream, the Gros Ventres suffered severely at the hands of their onetime friends, the Pecunnies,[1] who were armed with guns, Red-moccasin and a large following, including Wolf's cousin, Left-hand, revolted. They were determined to arm themselves with the white man's deadly weapon, Left-hand being especially vociferous.

"We are not consistent," Red-moccasin told the council or warriors. "We use the white man's knives and his arrow points. We, of today, have never used anything else. We have grown used to these things. Who among us could get along without them? Nobody! And yet the knives and the arrow points are made by the white men just as the guns are. Count our dead. Some of them would be living today

---

[1] See Foreword.—F. B. L.

if we had been armed with guns. Yes, and more of the Pecunnies would now be dead men if we had had guns. And count your horses. Do not forget to count your horses. Many of them are missing because our enemies had guns. Let us not be foolish. Let us be wise. I ask all who will follow me to gather up many good buffalo robes and trade them for guns and powder and balls. We need not trade for other things. We do not need the other things. Let all those who disagree with us remember that we can fight even the white man to better advantage if we are armed as he is armed. I have finished.''

Black-tongue, sagacious and yet devoutly believing in the warning of Wolf's medicine dream, saw that he could no longer control these men. Without waiting for other chiefs to speak, he said: "Red-moccasin has spoken the truth. There *is* inconsistency among us. Most of us *do* use knives and arrow points made by white men. They *are* better than our old ones. I used them myself until Wolf dreamed. Then I went back to the ways of our fathers; and I am getting along well enough. Our fathers were better, stronger men than we are; and there must be a reason for this. But we cannot agree upon the reason, or upon anything else, because men's hearts, eyes, and thoughts differ. And in some ways this is well for us all. If every man loved the same woman, one would have to climb over dead men piled around her to tell her of his love. There is, in every man, a little voice that speaks only to him. Who, besides the hearer, knows what this little voice says? Nobody! I say let every man listen to his own little voice, because these little voices never lead men into trouble. You say that you will trade buffalo robes for the white man's guns, his powder, and his bullets; but will you stop at these things, or will you go on and on until you eat fish, *The Under-Water-People*, because the white man eats them? I am growing old. I have seen many strange things. I know that the dream of Wolf, son of Horned-bull, is a warning sent to us by the *Mysterious Ones*. I know that our fathers would have listened to it. Some of us will listen even now. But if trouble comes because of your trading with white men, we who have listened will be with you in the trouble as long as we live. I will say no more."

Red-moccasin spoke again. "Black-tongue is wise and fair," he said, with feeling. "We *will* stop at guns and powder and lead; but these things we must have or be wiped out by our enemies. We need not be friendly with white men because we trade with them a little. I do not like white men. I shall never like them. I would willingly go to war against them if we had guns. When we go to the post to trade for weapons, let us all go together, those who agree, and those who disagree, so that we may be strong against our enemies; and let us go soon."

Wolf, who had listened outside the lodge, went to his bed with a heavy heart. "Do not grieve, my Son," his mother said, to console him. "*The Mysterious Ones* will not blame you if our people will not listen."

"But Black-tongue did not scold our people. He even made them laugh," Wolf answered, feeling that he had now lost his greatest supporter.

"Ah, Black-tongue is wise, my Son," his mother said, seriously. "He saw that he could not make the men listen to reason tonight. Who but a fool would try to turn the Big River in flood time, make it go back up the stream? Black-tongue is as immovable as a mountain of stone; and yet where he must go he will go merrily. He has not changed, my Son."

"Mother, how did you know my dream?" Wolf asked, sitting up to look into her eyes across the smouldering fire.

But before she could answer, Horned-bull burst into the

lodge. "The Pecunnies have stolen our horses," he said excitedly, seizing his bow and quiver of arrows.

Outside men were running in all directions, calling to each other in the moonlight. A few were mounted upon war horses that luckily had been tied to their lodges. Wolf's father, calling to a friend, dashed toward the lower end of the village. Wolf followed until he met Black-tongue, who was returning alone from that direction.

The old man was chuckling. "Guns did not steal our horses, my Son," he said. "Our young men are too sleepy to stand guard nowadays. Two of them were killed. The only horses left us are those that were tied to men's lodges. We are afoot, my Son, afoot. We shall have to use dogs now, as our grandfathers did. We cannot even follow the thieves."

This proved to be the literal truth. So cunningly had the Pecunnies worked that all the loose horses had been stolen, more than four hundred head. Nobody knew when they had been taken. The loss was staggering. The Gros Ventres could not travel now, could not even follow the Pecunnies. Men spat disdainfully over their left hands when the names of the luckless night herders were spoken. The situation was beyond belief. The tribe felt disgraced, and by the hated Pecunnies. The present location of the Gros Ventre village, near the Marias, the land of the Pecunnies, the Blackfeet, was embarrassing. The village could not move; the Gros Ventres could not even hunt buffalo without horses, and there were but fifty horses left to the tribe.

Chagrined and deeply angry, the warriors gathered in groups. Women hurried from lodge to lodge, talking excitedly of the loss of the horses and the danger of attack. Children, bewildered by the tribal calamity, wandered aimlessly about the village, hand in hand, their voices subdued in the bright moonlight. The loss of the horses seemed to have relaxed all restrictions. Wolf, returning from the lower end of the village, met Breath-feather in the shadow of a lodge. Confused by the sudden meeting, the girl turned aside, a flush that sent Wolf's heart leaping, reddening her cheeks.

"Wait!" he whispered, as though the word had been forced from his lips.

She stopped in the shadow, turning toward him, her flushed face averted. A war drum began beating in a lighted lodge across from them, on the far side of the village.

"Breath-feather!" Wolf whispered, touching her bare arm, a surge of passion sweeping over him. And then, as though forgetting the village, he tossed his robe over the girl's head and his own, a sudden resolution in his mind.

"Beautiful One," he whispered, her hot cheek against his own, "I am going to war alone. I go tonight. Nobody but you must know that I have gone. If I am successful, if I count coup, I will ask your father for you when I return. Are you willing, Breath-feather?" he asked, holding her tightly.

"Yes, Wolf," she answered, lifting th edge of the robe to look about them. "But be careful. Be cautious, Wolf. It is not wise to go alone to war. I must go now, Wolf. Let me go. Somebody may see us. I will watch for your return." Lifting the robe from their heads, the girl looked into Wolf's eyes. "Oh, be careful," she whispered again, and then she slipped away among the lodges.

Throwing his robe over his shoulder, Wolf stood still for a moment, his eyes lifted to the clear moon as though waiting for some sign. "Ah, Winds," he whispered, when a night breeze stirred his hair. "You are here. You will help me. I am not afraid."

Relieved, certain of success in his purpose now, he had taken only a step forward when he saw his cousin, Left-hand, lift himself up from the lodge shadow not twenty feet from where he had covered Breath-feather's head with his robe.

Such meetings were forbidden. Blaming himself, Wolf thought only of Breath-feather. He knew that Left-hand had witnessed his meeting with the girl. The fact that it had been purely chance would not save her from shame if Left-hand should talk; and watching his cousin walk away in the moonlight, he felt certain that the half-breed would talk. If Wolf could have gone directly to Red-moccasin and asked for Breath-feather, he would have acted immediately. But even if he had possessed horses to give the war chief for his daughter, Wolf was not yet twenty and had not counted coup, so that this course was not open to him.

Reaching his father's lodge, Wolf found it vacant. This suited his purpose. Hastily filling his quiver with arrows and taking several pairs of moccasins, the dressed skin of a wolf, a small heart skin of pemmican, and a rawhide rope, the boy stepped out of the lodge into the moonlight, heading westward over the wide plains toward black, bordering mountains that under the moon seemed to mark the end of the world.

Chapter 6

When morning came, the news of Wolf's absence spread among the lodges of the crippled village. Men wondered. Women laid their hands upon their mouths in astonishment. Not even Rain could answer the questions of curious ones. To avoid his fellows, Horned-bull, Wolf's father, went hunting antelope before dawn. At sunup Small-voice hurried to pay a visit to Black-tongue, smiling brightly at wondering women on the way.

Calling the old man from his lodge, Small-voice whispered her message. "My son has gone to war alone," she said proudly. "Help him, Black-tongue. Use your powerful medicine for Wolf, who has dreamed and is out against our enemies alone."

Black-tongue made no reply. Nevertheless, within an hour Small-voice was gladdened by the sounds of the old man's beating drum and his highly pitched voice singing his medicine song. This singing and drumming continued until the sun looked down through the smoke holes of all the lodges, making Small-voice content.

Fresh meat was already growing scarce in the village, most of the men having to hunt on foot. Rain, Wolf's brother, was hunting for deer along the river so that Small-voice, alone in the lodge, was pleased when Breath-feather called, bringing her work with her. Together they sewed buckskin with sinew thread, talking merrily without either mentioning Wolf's absence, each filled with wonder at the other's silence upon the subject which was uppermost in both their minds.

"Your hair is beautiful, Breath-feather," Small-voice said, lifting a heavy braid that fell over the girl's pretty shoulder. "And you have such fine eyes! I like eyes that do not dodge those of others," she added, perhaps thinking of the shifty eyes of her nephew Left-hand, the half-breed.

The girl's face flushed violently, her thoughts flying to her guilty meeting with Wolf the night before. Conscious of the woman's amused glance at her burning cheeks, which she felt had betrayed her, she turned away to pick up a piece of buckskin. "I've pricked my finger," she laughed, a little abashed, the hot blood receding from her cheeks. She guessed that Small-voice knew Wolf had told her of his venture. Nevertheless, he had asked her to keep his secret, and she would.

When the girl had gone, Small-voice sat for a time gazing at the lodge door, her kindly eyes misty with feeling. "Ah, she knows. Breath-feather knows. Wolf has told her," she whispered, her heart singing her son's love story. "And she is so beautiful, so honest," she thought fondly of Breath-feather, whose blushing innocence had told her so much.

Breath-feather's visit in Horned-bull's lodge had not left her abashed. Even thoughts of her blushing under the searching eyes of Wolf's mother did not long annoy her. The incident, while betraying her in a measure, had made known to Small-voice her true position with Wolf, and this without a spoken word. Ever since she could remember, she had held Small-voice in high regard. Now she loved her, perhaps because Small-voice had not appeared to notice her embarrassment in the lodge.

However, there was a real ordeal waiting for Breath-feather. And here her wit and spirit were tried to their uttermost. Going to the river for water, she met Left-hand, who had carefully planned to meet her there. He had not told of his cousin's meeting with Breath-feather, not only because he feared Wolf, whose following among the younger men was considerable, but because he knew that spreading the story would make both Breath-feather and her powerful father his enemies for life. Nevertheless, being deeply jealous of Wolf, hating him,.Left-hand now hoped to turn Breath-feather against his cousin by cunningly using his secret.

"There is a spring of clearer water, better water, behind that big rock," he said, pointing.

The girl, wearing a wreath of wild roses upon her head, hesitated, her kettle swinging over the water.

"I'll show you the spring," offered Left-hand, gallantly getting up from the grass where he had been waiting, his gaudy shirt seeming to clash with the green of the surrounding bushes.

"Here it is." He stopped beside a bubbling spring no more than a dozen steps from the river itself. And then, when the slender girl bent to dip her kettle, "My cousin, Wolf, talks too much," he said, ambiguously.

The girl did not at first show that she had heard, though she felt the hot blood flooding her cheeks as she bent lower over the spring. She knew now that her meeting with Left-hand was not chance, that the young man had waited for her by the river; but why? "Have you told Wolf that he talks too much?" she asked, mischievously, with a backward glance at the handsome young man as she lifted the filled kettle.

"Wolf has gone; nobody knows where. He left the village in the night," he said, his shifty eyes lighting amorously. "You met him last night. I saw him afterwards. I believe he was afraid that I might tell you," he said, implying that Wolf had told him of the meeting.

Startled, and yet greatly relieved by this last, the girl's composure returned. She knew that Wolf had told Lefthand nothing and that, even though the half-breed had somehow seen Wolf and herself together on the night before, he could not have been near enough to have heard their whispered words. And it was possible that Wolf had discovered his cousin's presence near their meeting place, that he had spoken to him, and that in his ignorance Lefthand might now believe that Wolf had run away, fearing exposure by the half-breed. Breath-feather reasoned that up to now the half-breed had not talked. She knew he was vain. Perhaps she might seal his tongue until Wolf returned. She would try.

"And Wolf ran *away?*" she asked, putting both contempt and indignation into her voice.

"Yes," said the half-breed, stepping nearer, caught by her counterfeit indignation. "And anyhow, he's a bad talker. I am not a talker, Breath-feather. I love you, Pretty-one. I am going to count coup. When I do, will you listen if I ask your father for you?" he hurried on, encouraged by the girl's pretended shyness.

"Oh, I think it must be wonderful to count coup. I should like to be looking on when you count coup," she said coyly, her lowered eyes watching her swinging kettle brush the green grass.

"But will you listen when I do count coup, Breath-feather?" he urged, trying to take her hand.

"Don't," she whispered, backing away. "Somebody will see us. When you have counted coup, I will answer you

43

quickly enough. I must go now. That is a beautiful shirt you are wearing. I have noticed it before. Hurry your coup counting," she finished over her shoulder, her eyes smiling.

Thoroughly pleased with himself, Left-hand, singing a love song, turned back to his seat by the river. He had not been certain that Wolf had seen him on the night before and had been a little doubtful that his cousin's absence was due to fear that he might talk. But now that Breath-feather had been so easily convinced that this was the cause of the young man's leaving the village so secretly, Left-hand became convinced himself. And even if his cousin should return to the village, Breath-feather would not now dare to tell Wolf that he, Left-hand, had spoken to her of their meeting because of her meeting with himself.

Breath-feather, frightened by her meeting with Left-hand, whom she disliked, and her dissembling manner toward him, left her kettle of water at the door of her father's lodge, climbing to the top of a high knoll back of the village, where she flung herself face downward upon the waving grass and flowers to laugh and cry hysterically. Left-hand would watch for her now, try to meet her. And she did not dare to offend him. Even though she knew that Left-hand might have talked, bringing shame to her and her parents, she hated herself now for having given him reason to believe that he interested her. In her anxiety to seal his dangerous tongue she had even flattered the half-breed. If Wolf should return, successful, the story of their meeting might never be told; but the chances of her lover's counting coup against the hated Pecunnies were not great. Why had the Pecunnies so suddenly begun their war against her people? The Gros Ventres and the Pecunnies and the other two tribes of Blackfeet had been friends longer than her father could remember. Now, without any warning, the Pecunnies had attacked the Gros Ventres.

The war would go on, perhaps forever, and perhaps Wolf would never return. If he did not return, could she listen to Left-hand, even to save her good name?

Not until the sun was sinking behind the mountains beyond the land of the Pecunnies did Breath-feather regain her calmness. As she sat up in the grass on the knolltop, her eyes wandered across the intervening rolling plains, scanning the courses of the streams marked by fringing cottonwoods, until they reached the far-off peaks themselves. And then, as though to reassure her of Wolf's return to the village, the snow-capped summits of the mountains took on the warm colors of an early summer's sunset, and Black-tongue's drum began again to beat down in the village, where the smoke of evening fires were just beginning to curl from the tops of the lodges.

Chapter 7

The village was far behind Wolf when the bright moon slipped from his sight over the black mountains in the West, leaving the sky sparkling with stars. There was no need for caution, no fear of lurking Pecunnies so soon after their successful raid. Striding fast, his eyes on a mountain peak, Wolf hoped to be well into the enemy's country by sunrise. Near midnight, reaching the Marias, he began following this river's course. The Pecunnies might be anywhere along this stream, so that when the first signs of morning appeared, Wolf crept into a thick patch of small quaking aspens to hide for the day. He had seen but few buffalo during the night, concluding that the herds had been frightened from the range by the swiftly moving Pecunnies driving so many horses. Another night's traveling might bring him close to the Pecunnie village. Today he felt safe and would sleep.

He had thought long and deeply of his chance meeting with Breath-feather, blaming himself for tossing his robe over her head without knowing positively that they were alone. He had acted without thought. If Left-hand told of their meeting, Breath-feather's shame would be deep. He believed that the half-breed would tell the story, that even now Breath-feather was suffering because of his indiscretion. There was nothing that he could do, except to be successful in his venture, to count coup against the Pecunnies. Unwrapping his medicine bundle containing the stuffed head and a strip of the feathered skin of a War eagle, Wolf invoked the aid of his medicine, whispered passionately to the Winds a moment, and then slept soundly until dusk.

When he awoke to the rippling of the Marias, he was as alert and cautious as a hunted wild beast, listening intently before he got to his feet. Then after a drink of water, he slowly ate some pemmican, waded across the Marias, and climbed a high knoll to look at his intended way in the growing dusk. A quiet herd of buffalo, making a black patch on the plains, and a few wolves were all that he saw. Not a breeze was stirring. So still was the world that he could hear the contented grunting of the buffalo bulls. Before he started down from the knolltop, a mallard duck sailed over his head, dipping sharply downward into the shadows beside the Marias. The moon would soon come into the sky now. Descending the knoll, Wolf began again to follow the course of the Marias River, keeping near to its fringe of trees and bushes throughout the night without seeing any sign of the Pecunnies. At daylight he hid away as before. For one more night he traveled, following the Marias River until the coming sun warned him to seek cover.

On the third morning, just as he was about to enter a thicket to hide, he heard a horse whinny. The sound sent his blood leaping. He was near the Pecunnies, perhaps too near. The enemy's dogs might get wind of him and alarm the village. He had just passed a high knoll that stood out from the river a little way. Its top was strewn with large stones, many bushes growing among them. Retracing his steps, keeping within the river's skirting timber until opposite the knoll, Wolf crept across the intervening open space and then cautiously climbed to the knolltop. The sun was not yet up when he had worked his way to a position between two large stones partly screened by bushes, which he carefully parted with his hands. A large band of horses was grazing within half a mile of the knoll under the eyes of a young Pecunnie. At first he did not see the village, partially hidden by the timber along the Marias; but when the sun came, he counted two hundred lodges. Beyond the village he could see another and larger band of horses. While he watched from the bushes on the knoll top, many buffalo runners set out from the village to kill buffalo. There was little cover on the knoll top. Warriors and boys riding for pleasure might discover him. A single movement of the bushes about him might be seen by the practiced eyes of some chance passerby; and yet to move now was dangerous. He must wait for night. While he waited, he would plan.

The day grew hot, the sun beating down upon Wolf's naked back until he could feel his skin parching. Twice before noon horsemen came near, and once the hunters started a herd of buffalo toward the knoll, themselves following a cloud of dust. But when Wolf believed the buffalo must certainly sweep over the knoll, they suddenly swerved away from the Marias, narrowly relieving him of the danger of being trampled to death. The afternoon on the knoll top was even more torturing to Wolf. The knoll was the home of scores of rattlesnakes, made fretful by his presence there. They had been lured by the sun's heat from their dens beneath the rocks. The slightest movement of Wolf's moccasined feet set them rattling threateningly.

Nevertheless, lying there on the knolltop, Wolf planned for the night. A long, low ridge extended from the knoll far out onto the plains. The nearest herd of horses was grazing on the slope of this ridge toward the Pecunnie village, the feeding animals working steadily up the slight incline toward the ridge's top. If the horses crossed the ridge, they would be out of sight from the village, even in daylight. The young warrior guarding the herd was no farther than three hundred yards from the knoll. The young Pecunnie, seated upon the ground with his horse cropping the grass about him, would be relieved at nightfall. If the new guard stationed himself in about the same position, Wolf determined to creep along the ridge, on its far side, until opposite the Pecunnie, then slip cautiously up the hill and kill him. This would have to be accomplished before the moon came because Wolf would need darkness in which to drive the horses over the ridge from the village. If he was successful in this, he intended to visit the village itself, to steal a war horse tied to some warrior's lodge, and perhaps count coup upon a Pecunnie warrior there. The killing and scalping of the Pecunnie horse guard would not count as a coup. Much as he desired to get away with the herd of horses, he was determined to win the right to ask Red-moccasin for his daughter, Breath-feather, by counting coup. If he succeeded in driving the horses over the ridge, he would leave them there, cross the Marias, follow the stream to a point opposite the nearest lodges, and then slip into the village before the moon came. He wished that he might await a later hour to enter the village, but he needed time, every hour of darkness if he hoped to get away with the herd of horses. He had traveled afoot during three long nights to reach the Pecunnies. He would require half as much time to get away from them on horseback.

Many times he went carefully over his plan, noting every detail of the ground over which he would have to travel in darkness. He even tried to count the horses which he intended to steal, more than two hundred of them. Most of them were Gros Ventre horses, too. One of them, a pinto mare, belonged to Red-Moccasin. She was fast and smart. He would try to get this mare into the lead when at last he started the herd toward the Gros Ventre village. She would know the way, sense what was happening, and help him. If the new guard, set for the night, should move the herd or station himself in a more difficult position, then Wolf would somehow have to meet the situation.

Late in the afternoon the buffalo runners returned to the village with many travois loaded with meat. Later on, just before sundown, a young warrior, highly painted, visited the horse guard near the knoll. Wolf heard their talking and their laughter, wondering if they laughed at the ease with which they had robbed his people. Just at dusk the same painted Pecunnie who had earlier visited the horse guard relieved him for the night, seating himself upon a robe he had spread not far from the spot so long occupied by the day guard himself.

Wolf watched this change of men with deep satisfaction. Scarcely had the day guard ridden away toward the village when Wolf, the young Gros Ventre, began slipping cautiously down the knoll. Once at the foot where the long ridge joined the knoll, he began to creep out along the ridge on the side away from the Pecunnie, two arrows in his bow hand. He had marked a spot by a stone that was exactly across the ridge's summit from the horse guard, reaching it while yet there was twilight. Stopping here a moment to rest and calm himself, Wolf began creeping up the slope, an arrow fitted to his bowstring, his muscles taut, his heart beating rapidly. At last he was near enough to the ridge's top so that by standing upright he could see the Pecunnie. He had gathered himself for this movement when a sudden puff of wind from the West struck his face. "Ah, you are with me, Winds. I will wait," he whispered, sinking down to his knees, his eyes upon the ridge's top.

And then, as though the Wind had wisely warned him to wait, Wolf heard the Pecunnie singing softly to himself, heard the warrior moving toward him up the other side of the ridge. He was coming! Rising, with ready bow, Wolf waited until the painted Pecunnie stood upon the ridge's summit against the sky. Then, bending his bow with all his might, he let his arrow go.

The Pecunnie did not cry out, sinking down upon the grassy ridge, the shaft in his heart. Motionless, the notch of another arrow upon his bowstring, Wolf waited a moment, whispering his gratitude to his Helpers, The Winds. Then, taking his first scalp, he slowly, cautiously drove the herd of horses over the ridge as he had planned.

But he must hurry now. Leaving the horses well bunched and quietly grazing beyond the ridge from the village, he crossed the Marias, stopping for a needed drink of water before making his way up the stream to a point opposite the nearest lodges. Time was precious. He dared not wait to reconnoiter. The moon would come. Wading the swift Marias, Wolf entered the Pecunnie village at its lower end, creeping in the deeper shadows until he found concealment in a thick serviceberry bush. Several drums were beating beside a bright fire in the center of the village. Now, before the moon came, was the time to go on, to creep among the lodges. Rising to his knees, parting the bush with his hands, Wolf felt the night Wind press his face. "Yes," he whispered fanatically, sinking down again, "you will tell me when to go on, O Winds. You will tell me."

In the darkness he unwrapped his medicine-bundle, took out his Eagle medicine, tying the talisman to his hair. "Oh, help me, Winds. Help me, all You *Who Live Without Fire,*" he whispered, his blood hot with eagerness. The drums were beating loudly now. The Pecunnies were dancing with the scalps of Wolf's people. He could hear their exultant cries, their wolf-like yelps, see their shadowy forms in grotesque contortions in the firelight, tall lodges reflecting the yellow flames. Gratefully Wolf's hand felt the Pecunnie scalp at his belt. Perhaps he would live to dance with it.

Suddenly he sank down into the bush, his heart leaping. A warrior, leading a horse, was coming toward the nearest lodge. Scarcely breathing, Wolf watched the Pecunnie tie the horse to a stake driven into the ground beside the tall, painted lodge and then walk rapidly away toward the scalp dance. Now was his time; now, before the moon came.

"Oh, Winds, where are you?" he whispered, standing up, his lean body bent eagerly forward. "Yes," he whispered, feeling a gust of Wind on his back. "Yes, I will go on."

Gliding through the shadows, his bow ready, Wolf saw that the tall, painted lodge was dark. And yet he knew that a woman or a child might be within it. Stopping in its black shadow, Wolf listened intently. The lodge was vacant. But he could hear low voices in the next lodge, women talking not twenty feet away; and out on the plains a wolf was howling near the dead horse guard. Walking cautiously halfway around the tall lodge, Wolf heard the talking more distinctly. The warm night had caused the visiting women to lift their lodge skin from the ground, propping it up so that the breeze might enter. He could not distinguish the forms of the talking women in the interior blackness, and yet he knew that if he stepped out of the lodge shadow the women would see him. The horse, tied in front of the tall lodge, was not in the shadow. The animal was in plain sight of the women. Nevertheless, there was no time to waste. The moon would come. He must be off.

Turning, he walked softly back to the front of the tall lodge, being deliberate in every movement so that the horse tied there might not be frightened, might not snort or pull back. Drawing the picket stake from the ground and taking hold of the rope, Wolf gently led the horse to him, into the shadow. Reaching out his hand, he caressed the horse's forehead, glanced anxiously at the eastern sky, and then slowly led the horse away to the Marias, carefully keeping the tall lodge between himself and the gaping hole made by the lifted lodge skin where the women were talking.

Once across the river Wolf stopped to listen and to put two half hitches upon the horse's lower jaw with the rope, noticing with a thrill that there were two eagle feathers in the animal's mane and two in his tail, proof of the horse's distinction and worth. Leaping upon his back, Wolf rode up the river, recrossing the stream behind the low ridge from the village where the herd of horses was grazing as he had left it. By carefully maneuvering, he worked the pinto mare into a leading place, slowly starting the herd toward the Gros Ventre village without exciting the horses. He did not press them for a time, letting them walk until they knew that they were expected to travel. Then, when the rim of the moon rose above the eastern horizon, he un-wound the rawhide rope from his waist, sending one end of it popping against the tail of the nearest laggard. Twice, thrice, the stinging rope end popped; and then they were off on a swinging lope which Indian ponies can keep for hours without tiring. Wolf, behind them on his stolen Pecunnie war horse, an enemy's scalp at his belt, felt no great pride in his accomplishment. Instead, he felt humbly grateful to his medicine, The Winds, even though he had not counted coup.

Chapter 8

Wolf knew that the loss of the war horse would be discovered when its owner returned to the tall, painted lodge from the dance and that this discovery might be made at any moment. But he had pulled the picket pin, as a spirited horse might have pulled it; and he had thrown the pin into the Marias, hoping that the owner of the war horse would believe the animal had grown restless, broken away, and gone out to the horse herd, which was under guard. Unless the discovery of the loss of this horse led the Pecunnies to investigate at once, the theft of the herd might remain unknown until daylight, which was all the time that Wolf required to get away. He had most of the night yet ahead of him. If the Pecunnies took up his trail at daylight, he could easily reach his people before they caught him. He had traveled but three nights to find the Pecunnies, and was now traveling back again more than twice as rapidly as he had walked. But if the Pecunnies gave chase immediately upon discovering the loss of the war horse, he would have to leave the herd and escape them if possible. His war horse was fast, though by the time the Pecunnies reached him the spirited animal might be too nearly exhausted to make a hard race for his rider's life.

Throughout the night, under the bright moon and even

after the moon had gone, Wolf kept the herd moving rapidly. Twice, to save his war horse from useless herding and rope lashing, Wolf permitted a weary animal to drop behind the herd, leaving it to follow or turn back as it pleased. At daybreak he gave the horses a rest, himself climbing a knoll to look westward for the Pecunnies. For one man, however skilled, to keep so many horses going at a rapid pace was a difficult task. The constant herding and rope lashing was tiring his war horse. Nevertheless, Wolf knew that he had been traveling nearly as rapidly as his pursuers could travel. The difficulty now would be getting the stolen horses going again after resting. Each moment urged him to hurry on, and yet, because he knew that he must rest the horses, he remained on the knoll top until sunrise, eating pemmican and searching the plains for the Pecunnies. Then he was off again, Red-moccasin's pinto mare quickly taking the lead. He had had no opportunity to see the horses in the herd, so that he had recognized none but the pinto mare. Now that the sun had come, he saw that all the animals were Gros Ventre horses, four of them his father's. Knowing that they were going back to their old range, these horses had been more than willing to travel, thus being of immense service to Wolf, who kept them going at a steady gait.

The day grew excessively warm on the rolling plains. By noon the horses, dripping perspiration, began to lag seriously. They needed another rest and water. Wolf knew that there was water just ahead. Gradually letting the herd slacken its pace, he finally stopped the horses in a grassy coulee, holding them from the water for more than an hour. Then, by pressing and lashing them, he prevented their drinking heavily, though the thirsty animals clung doggedly to the water hole.

By three o'clock Wolf was in Gros Ventre country, though

far from safety, since his people had but few horses. He had not yet seen the Pecunnies who must now be on his trail, riding fast. By four o'clock he could see the Gros Ventre village, could see the sentinels on surrounding knolltops. He saw these sentinels signal the village with buffalo robes: "The enemy is coming." Wolf understood the consternation the signals would cause in the village. Pulling up, he rode his weary horse in a wide circle; then, stopping, he signaled the watching sentinels with his robe.

"I've found the enemy," the circle riding said; and the robe, "Come to my aid."

But the wary Gros Ventre sentinels waited until Wolf drew nearer before relaying his message to the village, which was already stirring. Instantly warriors afoot and mounted, many of the horses bearing two riders, raced out on the plains to meet Wolf, who waited, singing the Gros Ventre song of victory.

The oncoming warriors, with Red-moccasin leading, took up the song. Pressing about Wolf, singing of his victory over the Pecunnies, they would have escorted him into the village if he had not stopped them. "Listen," he called, holding up his hand to quiet his excited tribesmen. "Let guards take these horses behind our village and hold them there," he said to Red-moccasin. "Let the rest of us go to Dry Coulee and meet the Pecunnies. They cannot be far away. We must hurry."

Turning to his brother, Rain, whose eyes were shining with pride, Wolf said: "Brother, lead my horse to the village. Tie him to our lodge. Feed him cut grass, but do not give him any water until he has cooled. He has traveled far and fast." Much as he had hoped to go with the others to Dry Coulee, Rain did his brother's bidding, setting out at once.

Keen for this chance of a battle with the hated Pecunnies

Red-moccasin sent ten men away with the herd; and then, taking Wolf up behind him on his horse, he rode straight for Dry Coulee, followed by eighty eager warriors mounted upon forty horses.

Dry Coulee, distant nearly an hour's ride, burdened as their horses were, is a deeply cut ravine running nearly north and south across the plains. Each year the water from melting snows cuts the coulee deeper, drying up during the early summer, leaving the coulee's bed littered with gravel and the roots of sage. Its western bank was now six feet high, cut nearly straight through the plains for miles. If the Pecunnies came, they would have to cross Dry Coulee, and, following the trail of so many horses, they would be likely to cross the coulee where Wolf and the horses had crossed it.

The sun was low when the Gros Ventres reached the crossing in the coulee, Red-moccasin quickly stationing his warriors, one on a rocky knoll top to watch for the Pecunnies, forty men, standing by their horses in the coulee. The rest were hidden immediately below the rim of its western bank, all naked excepting breechclouts and moccasins, and all of them out of sight from the plains.

There were but four guns in the party. To use them to best advantage, Red-moccasin stationed their owners at regular intervals among the warriors who were hidden below the coulee's rim. Not a head was to show itself until the watcher on the rocky knoll top dropped his robe. At his signal the warriors under the coulee's rim were to rise and strike, the ready horsemen to mount and charge the surprised Pecunnies, routing them by the very suddenness of the attack.

Scarcely had these arrangements been made when the watcher signaled, "The enemy is coming." Wolf's blood bounded with joy. His first pitched battle was at hand. Setting himself for a quick leap over the coulee's edge, two arrows in his bow hand and two between his teeth, he could scarcely restrain himself from looking over the coulee's rim. But Red-moccasin, the war chief, was speaking, his voice trembling with half-suppressed passion.

"The Pecunnies, who so wickedly broke the peace between our tribes, are coming," he said. "They have slain your fathers and your brothers. They have stolen your horses, putting you to shame. This is your opportunity to wipe out this shame, to avenge our dead. Let each warrior here look upon Wolf, the son of Horned-bull, who alone went to war against the Pecunnies; took a Pecunnie scalp, and took a war horse from the Pecunnie village, besides stealing nearly two hundred loose horses. Be as brave as this young man. Strike the Pecunnies so hard that if you die this day your sons will speak your name with pride. Steady all. I have spoken."

"Ahh! Ahh!" Wolf heard these sounds of approval from the warriors everywhere; and then began the chanting of war songs, low-pitched and fanatically wild. This chanting set Wolf's blood afire with fury. He trembled with eagerness.

"Silence!" Red-moccasin held up his hand. The chanting ceased. A horse snuffled, and then Wolf, whose eyes were upon the watcher on the knoll top, heard the pounding of many hoofs. His temples throbbed. As he set the notch of an arrow upon his bowstring, his fingers were cold, his muscles straining painfully. Then down dropped the watcher's robe.

With the wild Gros Ventre war cry Wolf leaped upon the bank in the faces of frightened, swerving horses, sending his arrows, one, two, three, four, into their riders before the Gros Ventre horsemen could scramble over the coulee's rim. So sudden, so fierce, had been the attack and so wild the war cries that the Pecunnies lost control of their horses, those behind crowding upon the ones ahead until some were overthrown. One pitched headlong near Wolf, who was instantly upon its rider. Snatching the fallen warrior's gun, Wolf actually lifted the Pecunnie to his feet, slapping his face with an empty hand, thus counting the most honorable of coups. But even as he slapped the Pecunnie, an arrow from some Gros Ventre bow ended the warrior's life.

The battle on the edge of Dry Coulee was fierce, short, and yet bloody enough. The Pecunnies, though outnumbering the Gros Ventres two to one, broke and fled, followed by the mounted Gros Ventres under Red-moccasin, who did not press them far. Not a Gros Ventre had been killed, though six had been wounded, Wolf, himself, being cut along the side by a bullet. Fifteen Pecunnies had been killed and scalped. Ten horses, two of them wounded, had been captured by the Gros Ventres. The Gros Ventre war cry was loud and long, the dancing wild. Charring sticks with fire, the warriors blacked their faces; and then, singing the song of victory, waving the scalps of the fallen Pecunnies, they set out for their village, most of them riding double as before.

When the singing procession was near the village, Red-moccasin, the cunning war chief, mounted Wolf upon a captured horse, placing him in the lead, before entering between the two long lines of people, the women on one side, the men on the other, all singing the tribal song of praise.

The scene was inspiring, the chanted praise song stirring even the blood of the singers. Wolf, with blackened face, the sign of victory, led the procession with eyes that glanced shyly about for Breath-feather. She was there, singing beside his mother, her slender hands clasped before her, her forehead painted red. As she met Wolf's eyes, the cheeks of the graceful girl reddened prettily. She smiled at her passing hero, knowing that his young heart had been made to sing by her presence.

Turning at the ends of the long lines, the victorious party charged back, firing the guns and waking the evening echoes with the Gros Ventre war cry. Then solemnly and alone, Red-moccasin rode between the adoring lines, reciting Wolf's adventures over and over until everybody had heard him.

"Hear ye, hear ye!" Red-moccasin called, again riding between the lines of people. "Wolf, the son of Horned-bull, now possesses the right to change his name if he wishes. He has counted coup. He may sit in our council of warriors. The council will meet at once. I have finished."

Now the warriors, both old and young, eagerly crowded about Wolf, who, instead of going to the council, as was his right, walked slowly toward his father's lodge with his adoring brother, Rain.

"Ho, Wolf, son of Horned-bull, will you lend an old man two of your many horses?" asked Black-tongue, stepping before the bewildered boy. "I must move and cannot carry my lodge on my back," he said, bending nearly double, groaning, as though carrying a heavy burden.

Men laughed at the old Medicine-man's pantomime. Wolf knew they would all be interested in his answer. "Help youself to the horses, Black-tongue," he said. "Take four of them that please you. And tell the council that Red-moccasin may divide the horses among the people, excepting the four which you may choose, and four that must go to my father. I will keep only the Pecunnie war horse for myself."

Black-tongue placed his wrinkled hand upon Wolf's shoulder. "I knew what you would say, my Son," he said, his expressive eyes now soft as a woman's. "Your heart is both brave and big. I will tell the council of your generosity; but why not speak, yourself?"

Wolf's childish fear of the old Medicine-man had long ago vanished. This had been replaced by deep respect. He could not let Black-tongue believe that his success had made him proud. He feared to be proud. "I am glad that I have a right to sit in council," he said, slowly. "Sometime I may wish to be heard there. But now, tonight——Black-tongue, it was not I who did this thing. *They* did it, my Helpers, The Winds and *Those Who Live Without Fire*," he finished.

"Ah, but *They* help only brave hearts, my Son, the unafraid," said the old man, slowly turning away.

Wolf and Rain stopped to admire the Pecunnie war horse tied beside their father's lodge, a prize that both appreciated as only Indians can. Hearing their voices outside, their mother called; and when Rain led the horse away for a second drink of water, Wolf entered to greet his mother. She set food before him with so much formality that he smiled. "Am I a visiting chief in my father's lodge that my mother treats me as she would a stranger?" he asked, playfully pulling a braid of her hair.

"Hark!" She held up her hand in the little firelight. A crier was riding through the village with a message from the council, his words not yet clearly distinguishable. "Ah," she whispered, her eyes shining, when the cries drew nearer, "the village will move in the morning, and with horses given its people by my son." Thus, by seeming to whisper only to herself, she answered Wolf's bantering question. Always it is the women of mankind who foster tradition.

The village had heard; Breath-feather had heard the crier's message. And yet Wolf dared not recognize the thrill that leaped to his heart. *Those Who Live Without Fire* would know if he harbored pride. "It was The Winds, my Helpers, who did this thing," he said simply, his faith in his medicine stronger than ever before.

When Horned-bull returned from the council meeting, Small-voice and Rain lifted the lodge skin from the ground, propping it up with sticks of firewood so that the evening breeze might cool the lodge. Wolf, speaking in a low voice that only his family might hear, told of his adventures without boasting, never forgetting to give all the credit to his Helpers, The Winds, answering many questions asked by his proud father, who sat beside him in the darkness.

"I have never known a braver deed than this of yours," said Horned-bull when the boy had finished his story. "You will be a great chief, my Son. I am proud of you."

"It was The Winds, my Helpers," Wolf said, spreading his bed robe in the dark lodge. "I am tired," he added, lying down to sleep.

Chapter 9

Because of the long way to Fort Union the Gros Ventres, followers of Red-moccasin in his determination to obtain guns, were going to trade at the newer post, Fort Benton, on the upper Missouri. This fort was well within the Pecunnies' country. Nevertheless, the Gros Ventres hoped to move speedily, avoid contact with the enemy tribe, quickly obtain the needed guns, and then, if necessary, fight the Pecunnies, who outnumbered them, even without the Bloods and Blackfeet.[1] Of the same stock as the Arapahoes, the Gros Ventres were even more warlike than the Blackfeet, the bitterness of broken friendship deepening their hatred of the Pecunnies until now many of the warriors were willing to fight the whole nation of Blackfeet.

When in the morning the Gros Ventres, of more than two hundred lodges, moved toward Fort Benton, mounted scouts kept far in advance of the travois, every precaution being taken by Red-moccasin to guard against a surprise attack, which was expected, since the Pecunnies would be smarting from their defeat at Dry Coulee. All the warriors, excepting the scouts, walked, those having horses leading

[1] There are three tribes in the Blackfeet Nation: Pikunis, Bloods, and Blackfeet.—F. B. L.

them to keep them fresh for possible battle. Wolf, mounted upon his Pecunnie war horse, was each day sent out with the mounted scouts under the leadership of Black-tongue. But the Gros Ventres met no interference, reaching Fort Benton without having seen an enemy.

Their coming was unexpected by the traders, who had learned of the battle at Dry Coulee. Besides this, the presence of the Gros Ventres at Fort Benton was embarrassing to the traders, since there was a Pecunnie chief within the fort's stockade when the Gros Ventres arrived outside. Fortunately, this Pecunnie chief, befuddled by trade whiskey, did not know of the arrival of the Gros Ventres. Nevertheless, he was bent upon leaving the fort to return to his tribe. This the traders dared not permit. Even if the Pecunnie got safely away, which was not likely, he would return with his tribe to fight the Gros Ventres. A battle between the Pecunnies and the Gros Ventres so near the fort would be sure to make one tribe or the other an enemy of the traders, and perhaps both. This would be bad for business. And yet what could the traders do with the visiting Pecunnie? If the Gros Ventres even suspected his presence within the fort, they would find and kill him in spite of the traders. However, prodigious flattery and trade whiskey solved the distressing problem, so that during the two days and nights the canny traders managed to keep the Pecunnie chief confined in a cabin within the stockade as an honored guest, so drunk that he could not stand.

Many of the Gros Ventres, believing that Wolf's dream was a warning against the tribe's friendliness toward white men, had come to Fort Benton not to trade but only to support their tribesmen who desired guns, Wolf being the leader of the adherents of his dream's warning. This band, numbering forty-five men of all ages, kept aloof from the stockade's gate, jealously watching to see that no Gros Ventre bartered for other goods than guns and ammunition.

Left-hand, Wolf's half-breed cousin, was admitted within the stockade with the first party of Gros Ventres. Greeting the surprised traders in good English, the young man was instantly in high favor at Fort Benton. The trader, one of the most unscrupulous employees of the American Fur Company, had known Left-hand's father; and now, upon meeting the son, he showed the half-breed great deference, seating him upon a buffalo robe spread near the flag pole, ordering a cannon fired in salute of his guest.

When the gun had belched a flat report to a half charge of powder, the trader mounted a cabin and from its roof harangued the Gros Ventres by pretending to speak only to his own associates, extolling the deeds of Left-hand's father, welcoming the shifty-eyed half-breed to the fort. "The white father of Left-hand is a wise man, a great chief, who can command ten thousand white soldiers with big guns to do his bidding," he said, waiting for the fort's interpreter to repeat his words in the Gros Ventres tongue. "Left-hand is my friend, because his father is my friend," he went on, "and from where the sun now stands Left-hand's enemies are *my* enemies. I am ready to go to war against them." Then, only to impress the listening Gros Ventres, he showered gifts upon Left-hand, among them a gun and an American flag, to the amazement of the half-breed's companions, who began to look upon Left-hand with more respect. When that night the half-breed remained within the stockade as the white trader's guest while the heavy gate was closed to all others, the young man's name was upon every tongue in the village. The white trader was powerful. He was Left-hand's friend.

Envious of Wolf, believing that his medicine dream had

placed the young man in high favor with the tribal chiefs, Left-hand was exultantly sensible to all the talk which the trader's deference had occasioned. Even during his entertainment within the stockade, the half-breed cunningly prepared to build upon his new popularity by cultivating the inherent superstition of the Gros Ventres. Having spent his life among both white men and Indians, he understood a little of the religion of both. He well knew that, while the white trappers and traders held their religion lightly, often denying any, the plains Indian was naturally a deeply religious man. He also knew that in his tolerance toward the religions of other men the plains Indian had measured the power of the white man's God by the visible attainments of the white traders and trappers and that he had come to believe Him the most powerful of all gods because of these attainments. He, Left-hand, would play upon this belief by pretending that he had been given a *medicine*[2] by the white man's God while in the stockade. And he would work upon the Indian's superstitious dread of offending the god of any man. But first, now while within the stockade, he must secure something that would represent his *God-medicine*, something that would seem strangely mysterious to the superstitious Gros Ventres. He knew that this ought not to prove difficult. The Gros Ventres had seen so little of the white man that nearly anything which was uncommon would answer his purpose. But the Gros Ventres would be likely to see more of the white man after this, and so become acquainted with his common things. He must be extremely careful. His *God-medicine* must not too soon lose its mystery.

When the buffalo tallow candle was lighted in the cabin inside the stockade, as though the devil himself were

[2] A charm, a talisman.—F. B. L.

fostering the half-breed's project, the entertaining trader talked of the foolish war between the Gros Ventres and Pecunnies, going so far as to tell Left-hand that Governor Isaac Stevens, "the Big White Chief of all the lands and people between the Mississippi and the Big Salty Water," was going to interfere, was going to stop the war. "Let this be a secret between you and me," he said, familiarly nudging the half-breed. "White men who are Little Chiefs will invite the tribes to a big feast at the mouth of the Judith River. All the chiefs of all the plains tribes will be there, and they will make peace. There will be no more war."

"When? When will the Little White Chiefs come to the Gros Ventres?" asked Left-hand, his crafty mind quick to see personal advantage in this information.

"Soon. Maybe fifteen sleeps. Maybe not so many. But do not talk. Let nobody know of this," warned the trader, sorry now that he had confided in the half-breed.

"I will promise not to talk. I will speak no word of this if you will promise not to tell any other man of my tribe."

"Good!" agreed the trader. "It's a secret between you and me then. I shall be with the Little White Chiefs when they come to the Gros Ventres, and I will pay you to be our interpreter when we talk with your people. Ho!"

Several times the trader had poured whiskey for Left-hand. Finally the half-breed became confidential, telling the trader of Wolf's dream and the consequent determination of most of the older warriors to avoid trading with white men, excepting for guns, ammunition, and arrow points. He boasted that he, the traders' good friend, would nevertheless bring the Gros Ventres to Fort Benton to trade twice each year. He told of Wolf's stealing two hundred head of Pecunnie horses, told of Wolf's stealing the Pecunnie war horse, and of his counting coup against the

Pecunnies. "But I am more popular than Wolf," he whispered drunkenly. "I am already a big chief. I am going to marry the only young woman that Wolf wants. Don't you tell this. Wait and see."

When he could learn no more from his guest, the trader led Left-hand to a cabin next to his own, opened its hewn door upon its heavy wooden hinges, lighted a candle, which he placed upon a crude table fastened to the log wall within, and then gave the half-breed a last swallow of trade whiskey—all with extraordinary flourishes which he knew would be mistaken for deferential hospitality. "This is the home of my good friend, Bateese Ladeau, who has gone on a visit into Canada. It is yours for tonight. I hope you sleep well," he said, bowing himself out, thoroughly satisfied with the evening. And why not? Left-hand's talking had decided the canny trader to double the price of guns, ammunition, and arrow points.

Alone in the Frenchman's cabin, Left-hand thought again of his *God-medicine*. He must get it tonight. But first he wanted a drink of water. His parched tongue felt like a chip in his mouth. Stepping outside, he made his way, staggering a little, to the fort's water barrel near the flagpole and shiny brass cannon which had so nobly saluted him. Dipping thrice, he drank greedily from an iron cup chained to the barrel, before dropping the captive cup, which rang noisily upon its chain. Beyond the embers of a fire near the brass cannon a disturbed wolf dog growled ominously, and a man lying upon a buffalo robe near the dog muttered in his sleep. Turning from the water barrel, Left-hand set his course for his cabin, which was marked by the candlelight streaming through its open door, his mind again on his *God-medicine*. Outside the tall stockade wolves were howling, and upon the balcony within, armed guards were walking back and forth beneath the night's stars.

As though the necessity for stealth had suddenly appeared, Left-hand softly closed the cabin door, smiling at thoughts of the fort's guards, who were so suspiciously watching the silent lodges of the visiting Gros Ventres, whose own guards were as carefully watching the plains for Pecunnies. Lifting the candle from the table where the trader had placed it, the half-breed calmly surveyed the cabin's contents, a broken gun, two steel traps, a battered axe, a pair of snowshoes, a roll of buffalo robes upon the bunk, and a painted elk skin sack that hung from a peg in a corner. The last caused Left-hand's eyes to light craftily. The sack was such as the white trappers called a "possibles an' fixin's bag," and might contain little treasures gathered by its owner. Replacing the candle upon the table, Left-hand took down the sack, carrying it to the light, where he eagerly untied its fastening thong, emptying the contents upon the table.

The cabin door was closed, and there were no windows. Left-hand was not in a hurry, carefully examining a small brass telescope, which tempted him; a steel for striking fire; several brass buttons; a dozen gun flints wrapped in buckskin; a small trade mirror; a file; a tinderbox; many buckskin needles stuck in rows in greased buckskin; some sinew thread; and a tiny, painted rawhide case which was about three inches wide and six inches long, opening at one end. With his thumb and finger Left-hand drew from this case a thin, black box of heavy wood, worn round at its corners by age. Its lid was not hinged, lifting off exactly as one lifts the lid from a modern pasteboard box. But so skillful had been the maker of this ark of ebony that for minutes Left-hand was uncertain whether it was indeed a box or a block of polished wood. Baffled, the slender fingers of both hands constantly working to discover the secret, if one there was, he was startled when suddenly the box fell apart, spilling upon the table a brass crucifix that had once been lightly washed with gold.

His *God-medicine!* Nothing could have better suited his purpose, and yet when he lifted the tarnished cross with its contorted Christ figure into the light, the flickering candle flame, the dark shadows about him, and his inherent superstition made him a little afraid. Without reason he went stealthily to the door to listen, the crucifix in his hand. Returning to the table, he hastily replaced the crucifix in its fitted place within the black box, slid the box into its painted rawhide case, and hid the case in his shirt.

Only one thing left upon the table tempted him. This was the brass telescope, so useful on the plains. But he did not take it. Replacing the coveted thing in the elkskin sack with the rest, he returned the Frenchman's bag of "possibles an fixin's" to its peg in the corner.

He would have fled now if the gates of the stockade had been open, but they were closed and guarded. He must stay in the Frenchman's cabin until morning, pretending to sleep. But first he wanted another drink of water. The embers of the fire no longer glowed near the brass cannon. Nevertheless, Left-hand easily found the water barrel, drinking hungrily. Voices came to him, angry voices, from a cabin against the stockade near the blacksmith's shop. Letting the iron cup down, this time without a sound, he glided across the intervening space to the cabin door, pressing his ear against a thin crack through which streamed a little light.

Pecunnies! Two of them! No, *one* Pecunnie, and a white man *speaking* Pecunnie. Quick thoughts of treachery on the part of the white trader chilled Left-hand's cowardly heart. And yet for another moment he held himself from useless flight, listening intently to Pecunnie words which he had instantly recognized without understanding their meaning. Suddenly the Pecunnie began to chant, to sing a war song. *Drunk!* The Pecunnie in the cabin was beastly drunk; his companion, the white man, was sober.

"Ah," Left-hand's heart began to beat normally now. He even smiled a little. Having been born in a white man's trading post, he knew exactly why the Pecunnie was so gloriously drunk and why he was so carefully confined in the cabin with the white man. This would be gladsome news for the Gros Ventres. They would wreck the fort, kill the Pecunnie, perhaps kill the white men. Should he tell the Gros Ventres that there was a Pecunnie in the stockade? By telling, he would strengthen himself with Red-moccasin and the warriors. Should he tell?

Sobered by his discovery, unable to decide what course he would take with his secret, Left-hand returned to his cabin, stretching himself upon the bunk. He knew that early in the morning thirty or forty Gros Ventres would be admitted within the stockade to trade. If these Gros Ventres knew that the Pecunnie was in the cabin near the blacksmith's shop, they would kill him even if they had to fight the white traders themselves. Should he tell the Gros Ventres in the morning or go to Red-moccasin himself, and tell him?

Sitting up in his bunk, he thrust his hand within his shirt for his *God-medicine*, his fingers closing upon the painted, rawhide case. Drawing it out in the darkness, he removed the lid from the black ebony box, bending low over the crucifix. "Shall I tell the Gros Ventres in the morning?" he whispered, conscious of something like faith in his *God-medicine*. Four times he whispered the question, his lips nearly touching the Christ figure on the cross. And then, "No!" he whispered, as though his medicine had answered, a cunning scheme clearly in his mind.

Chapter 10

The Gros Ventres began trading at sunrise, the exorbitant price in buffalo robes charged by the traders for guns failing to balk them. And this was always the way of the old-time Indian. Even though he was himself a natural trader, if he wanted an article and possessed its price, he satisfied his want without regret; and he was ever a judge of quality. However, even with the price so high, the Gros Ventres had by noon traded for sixty guns, many extra flints, and a large quantity of powder, balls, and arrow points, exhausting the supply of firearms at Fort Benton; anyhow so they were told. If there were yet more trade guns in the fort, the traders would not let the Gros Ventres have them, probably not wishing to thoroughly arm these tribesmen against their regular patrons, the Pecunnies.

Realizing that by their very presence at Fort Benton they were giving only a half measure of recognition to Wolf's warning dream, neither Wolf nor his followers had entered the stockade. Nevertheless, they found no fault, since the warriors who had traded had kept their promise, having purchased nothing excepting guns, ammunition, and arrow points.

While the first party of trading Gros Ventres was in the stockade, Left-hand returned to the village with his presents. These he dumped without ceremony at the door of his mother's lodge, sitting down with his head in his hands, his body swaying as though in agony. His mother, frightened by her son's actions, called another woman, who left her work, coming hurriedly to the stricken young man. But Left-hand, who continued to rock and sway his body, would answer none of his anxious mother's questions, thus increasing her fright. When other women, who had been taking down their lodges and packing for an early move of the village, came running to his mother's side, Left-hand began to roll upon the ground, his body doubled up as though suffering intense pain.

Wolf, Black-tongue, and several other men who had been standing outside the stockade's gate to watch the trading had not greeted Left-hand very warmly when he had passed them on his way to the village with his presents. But now, hearing excited voices and seeing the women gathered about the half-breed, they quickly joined the huddle.

"What is the matter?" asked Black-tongue, calmly pushing his way among the women to bend over Left-hand, whose forehead was shining with perspiration.

The cunning half-breed had waited for this moment. For a time he did not answer, continuing to groan and roll, one hand now beneath his shirt.

"Are you wounded?" Black-tongue took hold of Left-hand's shoulder, arresting the rolling. "Are you wounded?" he repeated, a little sternly.

At the old Medicine-man's touch Left-hand stretched himself face downward, and was still, his breast heaving painfully, his breath coming in quick gasps. Muttering incoherently, he turned over, sitting up, to look dazedly at those about him. "Ah," he sighed, brushing his eyes. "I

74

have dreamed. In the fort I dreamed a great dream. The white man's God gave me this medicine. See?" he asked, holding up the black, ebony box, unopened, his hand trembling with the intensity of his acting.

Relieved, the women fell back now, leaving him to the men, more than a score of them, all of them superstitiously impressed. Even though old Black-tongue may have been skeptical, he gravely helped the half-breed to his feet, leading him to the shade of a leafy cottonwood, where he seated him, Wolf and the others following.

Glancing right and left at the preparations for moving the village, Left-hand knew that his plan, formed the night before, would have to be changed. But he had so thoroughly given his mind to his recent acting that not until several young men drove the Gros Ventres' horses into a rope corral near the village could he command his thoughts. Nobody had told him the village would move so soon. He had intended to wait until night for his final acting. But the village would be gone before sundown. The traders would let the Pecunnie out of the cabin as soon as the Gros Ventres were safely away. The befuddled Pecunnie would immediately set out to find his tribesmen, who were somewhere northwest of the fort. Left-hand had planned to lie in waiting for the unsuspecting Pecunnie and from carefully chosen ambush kill him without danger to himself. But he must find his place of concealment, far enough away from the fort so that a shot might not be heard before the Pecunnie left the stockade. There was no time to be lost.

"Yes! Yes!" he said, suddenly, lifting the ebony box, both hands clutching it tightly, his body tense. "Yes!" he repeated, rising to his feet to bend eagerly over the box. "Yes, I will do as you tell me. I will come. I will come!" And then, without even a glance at the men clustered about him, he ran to his mother's lodge; snatched up his gun, powder, horn, and bullet pouch; and left the village, running wildly up the river.

Amazement held the men grouped by the cottonwood tree as though they were fettered there. So perfectly had the half-breed acted the part of a man under the influence of the mysterious power in which they all believed that Wolf and Black-tongue stood staring into each other's eyes without speaking. They distrusted the half-breed. Doubt must have been in the thoughts of both, and yet neither spoke, perhaps fearing possible offense to *Those Who Live Without Fire.*

At last, as though thoughts of the lone half-breed's danger in going farther into the enemy's country had broken the spell that had been upon him, a tall warrior touched Black-tongue's shoulder. "Left-hand will be killed," he said. "Let us go after him. Let us bring him back."

"Maybe he is crazed, not in his right mind," offered another, a young man who looked upon Wolf as his leader.

"If Left-hand is crazy, *Those Who Live Without Fire* will care for him," said old Black-tongue, positively. "If he dreamed and the white man's God gave him the medicine that called him away, he will not be killed. Let no man follow Left-hand. If the half-breed's heart is good, if his tongue is not forked like that of a snake, he will return to us. If he has lied, *They* will punish him with death. See," he pointed, the trading finished. "We shall now move eastward."

Loaded travois were already leaving the camping ground, Red-moccasin sending mounted guards ahead of them, and yet others to guard the flanks of the moving village. Calling to Black-tongue and Wolf, the war chief detailed them, with others, to guard the rear against a surprise attack, himself remaining with this most important detachment until the last travois had been gone half an hour, listening without comment to Black-tongue's account of Left-hand's strange actions. Finally the chief sent out his rear guard scattering the men widely over the plains, himself keeping the center.

By the time the Gros Ventres were well started upon their way to their own territory, Left-hand had reached the point above Fort Benton where the Teton swings down nearest to the Missouri River. Here the two streams are very near each other; and just here the Pecunnie trail, marked plainly by the tribe's trading expeditions during the several years since the fort had been established, turned north to cross the Teton. Large cottonwoods grew on the intervening plains, and at the crossing of the Teton there were clumps of alders, quaking aspens, and willows, particularly on the side toward the Missouri. Reaching the Teton, Left-hand carefully examined these clumps of bushes, at first selecting the one growing nearest the trail at its entrance to the water. But this selected clump grew on the trail's upper side. By sundown the wind would be blowing from the westward mountains, down the Teton. If Left-hand hid himself in this clump, the Pecunnie's horse would smell him before entering the water. Even with his advantage over the lone Pecunnie, who had been so long drunk on cheap trade liquor and must now be in a shaken condition, the half-breed dared not risk a fight with the Indian. Reluctantly giving up his first choice of bush clumps, Left-hand settled himself in a thick patch of willows farther from the crossing but on the trail's lower side.

The sun went down, the plains taking on the purple of evening. The expected breeze blew freshly down the Teton, bringing the odor of sweet sage and deeper shadows; and yet the Pecunnie did not come to the crossing. Once Left-hand cocked his gun at the sound of hoofs; but

77

they were buffalo across the ford. Again, when the stars had grown bright overhead, he saw a band of graceful antelope drink at the far side of the crossing; but during all the short northwestern summer night he saw nothing else, heard nothing else, save only the howling of wolves north of the Teton. All the warm night the soft breeze blew from the west, down the Teton; and then, when the eastern sky brightened, the wind came to Left-hand from the east, blowing *up* the Teton. With its first breath he moved to the willow clump he had first chosen, settling himself with a feeling that success would now come to him. He had not waited long in the bushes above the crossing when he heard a horse coming. Priming the pan of his flintlock gun, Left-hand parted the willows, looking through a leafy opening. The Pecunnie was coming, his head bent forward as though half-asleep, his horse trotting steadily along the trail to the crossing in the fast-growing light.

Left-hand, afraid of the unsuspecting Pecunnie, prepared to steady his aim with a rest stick pressed against his side at the hip, the fore end of his short flintlock trade gun resting in the crotch between the thumb and forefinger holding the stick. He dared not miss.

The Pecunnie was abreast of him now, not more than fifteen paces distant, the odor of the sweating horse strong on the morning wind. Holding his fire, the half-breed waited until the horse, stepping into the water, stopped to drink. Then the flintlock's ounce ball tore through the Pecunnie's left side below the shoulder blade, pitching him sidewise into the shallow water. His horse, leaping ahead, dragged the long rawhide rope, which was around his neck and half-hitched to his lower jaw, halfway across the stream before stopping.

Dropping his gun, Left-hand drew his knife, leaping from his cover to run into the Teton after the dragging rope, securing the horse. "Ho!" he exulted, bending over the Pecunnie to viciously slap the dead man's face, as though counting coup. Hastily taking his scalp, gun, powder horn, bullet pouch, and robe, Left-hand mounted the Pecunnie's horse, crossing the north bank of the Teton to ride rapidly down that stream.

The dead Pecunnie would soon be discovered in the shallow water at the crossing. This killing, so near Fort Benton might bring trouble to his good friend the white trader there. However, now that Left-hand felt assured of his future leadership of the Gros Ventres, he gave this little thought. The Gros Ventres would now believe that he had actually dreamed and that his *God-medicine* was powerful. He would use it to build greater power for himself. He would tell the Gros Ventres that he had counted coup upon the Pecunnie, first slapping his face before killing him. And he would say that the Pecunnie was riding toward Fort Benton from the north, that his *God-medicine* had told him the man was coming to the post. Nobody could prove that this was a lie. Black-tongue and Wolf, and many others, would believe that his *God-medicine* had called him from the village. He knew that his acting had been perfect; and now having counted coup, he would have the right to ask Red-moccasin for Breath-feather. Thoughts of possessing the beautiful girl, thus defeating his cousin, Wolf, who loved her, thrilled his cowardly heart. He hoped to overtake the village before night. He would enter it with his face blackened, singing of victory. There would be rejoicing in the village. The people would gather, sing the Praise Song, when he rode among the lodges on the dead Pecunnie's horse. Everybody would notice that he had the Pecunnie's scalp and that he carried two guns, two powder horns, and two bullet pouches. Wolf would be envious.

Long before noon Left-hand had crossed the Marias, which turns abruptly south to empty itself into the Missouri soon after receiving the waters of the Teton. Here he struck the trail of the moving Gros Ventre village, feeling comparatively safe, passing the Gros Ventres' last night's camping place by two o'clock.

Here he blackened his face with a charred stick from a Gros Ventre fire. And yet, when he entered the village, there was no rejoicing, no singing. The village itself was without form. None of the lodges had been pitched. The Gros Ventres, fearing that the Pecunnies might have enlisted the two other tribes of Blackfeet against them, were traveling rapidly to reach their own territory and would again move at daylight.

Nevertheless Left-hand's coming caused a stir. Men gathered to hear his story. He told it vividly, often mentioning the power of his *God-medicine* which had so suddenly called him from the village near Fort Benton. Displaying the Pecunnie's scalp, gun and horse, the half-breed enacted his coup counting, in his excitement slapping the face of a young warrior, causing much merriment.

Black-tongue, who had been minutely examining the Pecunnie horse, returned to the group gathered about Left-hand. "You say that you waited for the Pecunnie on the *south* side of the Teton crossing, and on the *upper* side of the trail?" he asked, blandly.

"Yes, I have twice told you this," snapped the half-breed, feeling certain that his story had been believed.

"I have not forgotten, but which way was the Pecunnie riding when you shot him, *toward* the white man's fort, or *away* from it?" asked the old man, unruffled by the half-breed's show of temper.

"*Toward* the fort, *Wise-one; out* of the Pecunnie country." Left-hand's voice was needlessly loud now. "Would a lone

Pecunnie be a visitor at the white man's fort with our people, the Gros Ventres? Have you lost your wisdom, Black-tongue?" he asked, contemptuously, walking to his horse.

Black-tongue followed him. "And yet you shot the Pecunnie in the *left* side, and a little *behind*,: he whispered, his hand on the half-breed's shoulder. "Wash the blood from the horse before you tell your story to the council, young man. It's on the wrong *side*," he said, his good natured voice scarcely audible, his eyes twinkling.

He despised the half-breed, burned to expose him immediately. But even though he knew that Left-hand had lied about counting coup on the Pecunnie, he had been impressed by the young man's strange actions in the village near Fort Benton, reasoning that if Left-hand had been called from the village by his *God-medicine* he possessed powerful Helpers; and the old medicine-man dared not offend *Those Who Live Without Fire*. He would wait for a time, carefully watching Left-hand. If the half-breed dared to press his claim to the coup before the tribal council of warriors, he, Black-tongue, would denounce him there.

Chapter 11

Breath-feather had found no opportunity to talk with Wolf since his return to the village with the Pecunnie horses. She was anxious to tell him of her meeting with Left-hand and to confess her pretended interest in the half-breed. And yet convention forbade her seeking Wolf, who was now in high favor. She had heard her father, Red-moccasin, praise Wolf in their lodge, even telling the thrilling story of the young man's bravery in the battle with the Pecunnies at Dry Coulee. Nevertheless, her father's high opinion of her lover's prowess only increased her anxiety for Wolf to ask for her in marriage, now that he had counted coup. She was nearly nineteen. Any day now her father might promise her to some other man. She knew that he was ambitious, that he would give her to any warrior whose notoriety might add luster to his own leadership. She feared Left-hand's growing popularity. Already the half-breed's *God-medicine* was the talk of the tribe. If the council acknowledged that he had counted coup, her father might easily listen to Left-hand's proposal.

There was yet another reason for Breath-feather's anxiety. She had a married sister. If this sister's husband should demand her as his second wife before her father bestowed her upon another, she would belong to him by tribal law.

However, this last did not trouble her greatly. Her sister's husband was already an old man, besides being a poor provider. It was Left-hand who worried her. When would he appear before the council of warriors? she wondered.

On the day following Left-hand's return to the village with the Pecunnie's scalp and horse, Breath-feather walked nearly all day with Small-voice, Wolf's mother. She had hoped to see Wolf, to talk with him. But both Wolf and his brother, Rain, were absent. Wolf had been detailed to guard the moving tribe's rear, and not once did she see him. Small-voice, deeply fond of the young woman, and wise, talked merrily as together they trudged beside the heavily laden travois. Sometimes, and, as the day grew old, often, the two women looked back to the rolling plains; and yet, even when the hot sun had set and camp had been made, they had seen neither Wolf nor Rain. All the others, the warriors who had been detailed to scout ahead, and to guard the rear of the moving tribe, had come to camp; none of these men had seen Wolf or his brother since morning.

"He will come. Wolf will come tonight." Small-voice spoke softly, and yet with a certainty that lifted a burden from Breath-feather's heart. "He has dreamed," she whispered, as the girl turned to leave her. "Wolf has powerful Helpers. He will come tonight."

She had made her eyes merry. Her lips had even smiled. And yet, when Breath-feather had gone, Small-voice, turning, gazed fixedly at the reddening sunset sky as one who must face an ordeal. Rigid, her lips parted in fearful anticipation, she watched the colors deepen and die; then, as though they had confirmed some terrible message, Wolf's mother cut off a braid of her hair. "Oh, Rain! Rain, my son," she sobbed, covering her face with her robe.

She was wailing, as only Indian women wail for their

dead, when Horned-bull came to her. "What is this, Woman?" he asked, his heart heavy with foreboding. "What is this?"

It was not Small-voice who answered but Wolf, himself, wild-eyed and suffering from deep scarifications. "Oh, my Father, Mother, Rain is dead, scalped, and all because I played the fool," he said, his voice hollow with agony.

"No! No!" Small-voice put both her hands upon Wolf's bleeding shoulders. "You did not play the fool, my Son. You could not have prevented this, this awful blow. It was to be. It was to be. Oh, I know. I know," she finished, sinking down to wail beneath the softness of her robe. Men and women gathered round the stricken family, listening in deep silence to Wolf's story.

"It happened a little below the place where you crossed Eagle creek," he told them, looking steadily into the pitying eyes of Breath-feather, whose arm was about his mother's waist. "I was walking, leading my Pecunnie war horse, with Rain walking a little behind me," he went on as though his words seared his lips. "We had seen running buffalo from a knoll top, and there we stopped, watching the plains for a long time. But we saw no Pecunnies, no hunters. The running buffalo crossed Eagle Creek above the point where you people crossed it. I foolishly believed that if hunters had made the buffalo run they were Gros Ventres who had stopped to hunt for meat. We were far behind you now, so far that I had seen no Gros Ventre guards for a long time when we reached Eagle Creek.

"Rain and I were thirsty. We stopped to drink. While I was drinking, Rain said that he believed he had heard a shot from a gun. I heard no shot. 'Which way was the sound?' I asked Rain. He pointed across Eagle Creek and a little down the stream. The Big River was not far away. I could see tall cottonwoods near the point where Eagle

Creek joined it. 'Hold my horse,' I said, running along the bank of Eagle Creek to a tall tree. Leaving my bow and quiver of arrows on the ground beside it, I climbed the tree so that I might better see the country. Scarcely had I reached the higher branches when I saw the bushes shaking near the point where all of you crossed Eagle Creek, where Rain and I had stopped to drink. I could see nothing that had made the bushes shake. I could not even see Rain. I climbed higher, and while I was climbing, it happened. From the bushes across Eagle Creek a Pecunnie killed Rain. The quick noise of the gun nearly stopped my heart. In my haste to reach my brother I nearly fell from the tree.

"Rain was dead, scalped; and the Pecunnie was gone. He had stolen my horse. I could not overtake him. But I saw him, saw him plainly when he turned on the horse to look back. He has only one eye. I shall know him, and I will kill him. I will dance with his scalp. Who will go with me?" he asked, eagerly scanning scores of grim warrior faces.

Thirty young men instantly volunteered, crowding about Wolf, all eager to go to war against the Pecunnies, openly hailing him as their leader. As their enthusiasm grew, ten more young warriors, chanting a war song, joined the others. The older men began to talk among themselves now. A new chief had risen. Red-moccasin, the tribe's war chief, hastened to the gathering war party, which had now withdrawn to the outskirts of the village. Wolf was speaking when Red-moccasin arrived. "We will leave as soon as I bury my brother," Wolf said, speaking rapidly. "We will go afoot, and before daybreak. Let each of you bring three pairs of moccasins and enough pemmican to last ten days. I will carry the pipe. Meet me before daybreak at the point where you crossed Eagle Creek today. I have finished."

"Wait! Wait!" Red-moccasin called, as the young men

moved away to make their preparations. "Wait, young men," he said, good-naturedly. "I am not an old woman. It is often well to go to war. We need horses, many horses. We shall get them from our enemies. Wolf, who will carry the pipe for you, is a wise leader, and he is brave. Besides this his heart is bad for our enemies, the Pecunnies. They have killed his brother. He will not rest until he has shed Pecunnie blood for this. I do not blame him, will not try to stop him. But I ask him, and I ask you who look upon him as your leader, to listen to me now.

"I have been told by one who has dreamed that within ten days from now White Chiefs will come to us and that these white men will come from the Great White Chief of all the lands and the people between the Mississippi River and the Big Salty Water, which lies far in the West. The dreamer has told me that these Little White Chiefs who will come to us will ask us to meet the Great White Chief at the mouth of the Judith River. He has said that the chiefs of all the tribes will be there, that all will make a treaty, and that there will then be no more war. Besides this, the dreamer has told me that the Great White Chief will give us many, many things, many horses, many guns, and a big feast, and that there will be much dancing.

"If these things are true, they are good. The Pecunnies greatly outnumber us. If the Bloods and Blackfeet join them, we cannot stand against them. We shall be killed or driven out of this country if we have to fight the whole Blackfeet nation.

"You have listened. Now I will make you a promise, and you know that I speak with a straight tongue. If these things which the dreamer has told me are lies, we shall know within ten days from now. If the Little White Chiefs do not come within ten days, all the Gros Ventres will go with you to war against the Pecunnies. Will you wait ten days?"

When he finished speaking, Red-moccasin was looking straight at Wolf, who knew that he must not show either subserviency or weakness before the young warriors who had so eagerly espoused his cause. And yet, in spite of his fevered desire to quickly avenge his brother, he had been impressed by Red-moccasin's words. Silently invoking guidance from his Helpers, Wolf stood facing at the darkening sky about his war chief's head until he felt the evening breeze behind him, upon his neck and bloody shoulders. It was pushing him toward the chief. This was enough. "Yes," he said to Red-moccasin, "I will wait ten days."

The young warriors dispersed, some of them feeling keen disappointment. Nevertheless many, nearly all, of them marveled at the dream. The day of its fulfillment or failure was so near that they were thrilled with anticipation. Surely somebody must have had a great medicine dream to have foretold such an event as this and to have set the date of its coming so near. But who was the dreamer? Who had told Red-moccasin that the Little White Chiefs were coming to talk to the Gros Ventres? Nobody could answer. If Wolf wondered, he gave no sign. He would wait ten days before going to war. Then, if he must, he would go alone against the Pecunnies.

It was past midnight when, all of them walking, Wolf led his sorrowing father and mother to his brother's body. Together they carried it a mile down Eagle Creek and then, after wrapping it in buffalo robes, fastened it securely upon a pole scaffold in a cottonwood tree. This done, each went alone onto the plains and knoll tops to mourn. During four days and nights they ate nothing, saw nothing of each other, cared not what might happen to them, Small-voice wailing aloud until, exhausted, she stumbled and fell unconscious upon the plains.

Wolf had crossed Eagle Creek when he left the burial

tree, walking blindly along the stream to the Missouri River. He could not have told the course he had taken after leaving the tree, scarcely noting the hours of daylight and darkness for four days and nights. Not until the evening of the fourth day did he think once of himself or his future. Now, turning toward the village which he had left, he thought first of his mother. If she did not soon come to the village, he would search for her. Perhaps his father would bring her in. He knew that the tribe had moved, that by now all the lodges were pitched in a more permanent place, and that he could easily follow and find them. The waning moon was up when he reached the dead fires of the village which he had left to bury Rain. Somebody had pitched his mother's lodge there. And somebody had picketed his father's four horses on good grass not far from the lodge. Wolf ate sparingly, intending to rest a little while before setting out with the horses to look for his parents. The comfortable lodge, and its neatly arranged equipage, brought new remembrances of his brother, and yet Wolf's mind was now trying desperately to steady itself so that he might comfort his mother. He thought tenderly of Breath-feather. Perhaps she had pitched the lodge and staked the horses. He would ask Red-moccasin for Breath-feather when a moon had passed since his brother's death. He had seen her on his way out of the village to bury Rain. Her back had been turned toward him in the evening light. And now he suddenly remembered that his cousin, Left-hand, had been sitting beside her father, Red-moccasin, that the two men were smoking together. Breath-feather's back had been turned to the smokers, perhaps intentionally.

The old moon was low and bright when Wolf left the lodge, riding one horse and leading two others. His mind was clear now, and he could see far. But there was nothing in sight on the rolling plains, not even a buffalo wolf.

When he was more than halfway to Eagle Creek, Wolf rode to the top of a knoll. Beyond its shadow, toward Eagle Creek, he saw his father and mother coming. They were walking together. With whispered thanks to his Helpers, Wolf rode to meet his parents. Before the moon had set, the three were lying upon robes in the lodge.

"We shall move in the morning," Wolf said, when his parents had lain down. "We must travel fast and find the village."

"Yes," agreed his father. "We will move in the morning. We will find the village."

There was no more talking. Unlike some of the other tribesmen of the great plains the Gros Ventres did not exclude the names of their dead from their conversations. And yet tonight, even though the thoughts of the three in the lodge of Horned-bull were of Rain, his name was not spoken. Rain was now a part of the Unknown, the Insolvable Mystery. His name was sacred.

Chapter 12

The Gros Ventre village was on the north bank of the Missouri not more than a day's travel above the mouth of the Judith River when Wolf and his parents found it. Even before they entered the great circle of lodges, they felt the excitement of their tribesmen there. Men, clothed in their finery and feathered bonnets, were riding in a parade about the village; there was song, and the beating of drums. Young warriors, painted and joyous, hastened to greet Wolf. "The Little White Chiefs have come," they said. "The dream has been fulfilled. The council has met, and we are to go to the camp of the Great White Chief at the mouth of the Judith in four days."

Somehow, even with his deep reverence for dreams, Wolf had not believed that the white men would come. Perhaps the blow of his brother's death, and his anxiety to avenge it, had made him skeptical of the dream. Now the white men were here in the village. "Who is the dreamer?" he asked, his mind recalling Red-moccasin's words.

"Left-hand," they told him. "Left-hand had this great medicine-dream. Everybody is talking of it. Last night after the council meeting Red-moccasin, leading Left-hand's horse, with the half-breed astride of the animal, walked about the village telling all the people of the dream and Left-hand's powerful medicine which was given him by the White man's God. Left-hand is going to act as interpreter when we meet the Great White Chief at the mouth of the Judith," they added, deeply impressed.

"There they are now!" said one of the young warriors, pointing to Red-moccasin and Left-hand, who were walking rapidly toward a painted lodge pitched in the center of the village. "They are going to visit the Little White Chiefs. Left-hand will talk for Red-moccasin," he added, turning to follow the war chief and the half-breed, hoping to catch part of the conversation from outside the painted lodge. The others followed, as though interested against their wills, to join in the eavesdropping.

Wolf, left alone, had no feeling that he had lost any of his following. Nevertheless, he was amazed at his cousin's evident power over Red-moccasin. The war chief and Left-hand appeared to be constantly together now. The half-breed, claiming to have counted coup, might ask Red-moccasin for Breath-feather. This thought had never before entered Wolf's mind. Even now he did not give it serious consideration. However, he determined to ask for Breath-feather himself as soon as he properly could.

His mother's lodge was pitched by this time, and yet it had not been pegged to the ground. Small-voice, as though intentionally delaying the pegging, was slowly moving the family goods inside. "Wolf!" she called softly, pointing cryptically to the lodge's doorway, which had not been covered by the hanging door flap.

"Yes," he answered absently. But as he started toward the lodge, old Black-tongue stopped him, his eyes twinkling.

"The dream has come true," Wolf said, thinking again of the possibility that Left-hand might ask for Breath-feather.

"Yes," agreed the old medicine man. "The white men have come. And yet I do not believe that Left-hand dreamed."

"Why do you say this?" asked Wolf, knowing that the old man had not spoken idly.

"Because the white trader, the trader who was at Fort Benton when we were there, came here with the White Chiefs. It was this same trader who gave Left-hand so many presents. It was he who kept the half-breed all night in the fort. I have seen them together here, seen them walking alone. I have heard them whispering together even though nobody else could have understood their spoken words if they were shouted. Why this whispering among people who do not know the whispered language? The trader must have known that these White Chiefs were coming to see us, must have known that the Great White Chief would meet all the tribes at the mouth of the Judith. Such events require time and much planning. I feel certain that when Left-hand stayed all night with him in the fort the trader told the half-breed and that the cunning cheat made use of the information by pretending to have had a medicine-dream. His dreaming is like his coup counting, a lie. But the people believe in him," he said, spitting scornfully over his hand.

"Do you *know* that he lied about counting coup on the Pecunnie?" Wolf asked, thinking again of Breath-feather.

"Yes, I *know* it," said Black-tongue, positively.

"Then why do you not speak, denounce him before the people?" Wolf asked eagerly.

The old man smiled craftily at his young friend. "Wolf, my son," he said slowly, "Left-hand's popularity is suddenly strong. It is like a fierce wind that holds wise men within their lodges. No man's voice can be heard far against a gale. But such winds do not last. The stronger they blow the quicker they die. I will wait," he ended, walking away.

"Wolf!" Small-voice, who had been anxiously waiting until the two men finished their talking, called again and again pointed covertly to the open lodge door.

"Yes, yes, Mother," Wolf answered, and then, stepping inside the lodge he met Breath-feather there alone.

"She, your mother planned this," whispered the excited girl as Wolf drew her into his arms, conscious that his watchful mother was now busily tying the flap over the doorway.

"Oh, Wolf, I am afraid of Left-hand." Breath-feather's whispered words were tense, fast, her frightened eyes on the unsteady door flap over Wolf's shoulder. "He waited for me beside the river," she went on, half-freeing herself from his arms. "He met me there, tried to make me believe that you had told him of our meeting on the night you went away. He must have seen us together. He said that he would ask my father for me. And Wolf, he will, he will! Oh, don't let——"

Small-voice thrust her arm through the doorway. Wolf felt Breath-feather start, tearing herself free. And then the girl was gone. Lifting the unpegged lodge skin opposite the dooorway, she had crept outside.

"Yes, Black-tongue, my son is in the lodge. He may be changing his moccasins," Wolf heard his mother say.

"Come in! Come in, Black-tongue," Wolf called, untying the strings of his moccasins, smiling at the sounds of busy pegging at the back of the lodge, where Breath-feather was helping his mother.

"Our talking about the dreaming half-breed made me forget my errand," began the old man, seating himself beside Wolf. "All the chiefs will speak at the meeting at the mouth of the Judith River. We all know that if the Bloods and Blackfeet join the Pecunnies against us we cannot live here and forever fight the whole Blackfeet nation. Because of this, and not because we love the Pecunnies, we believe that peace among all the tribes will be good. We could then sleep without feeling that before morning came we might have to fight before eating breakfast. You are already a young chief. Your voice should be heard at the peace meeting. Will you speak there, my Son?"

Wolf hesitated. He had never made a speech, had never even attended a council meeting. Besides this, he remembered that his cousin, Left-hand, was to interpret the speeches. He feared the half-breed's interpretation.

"It would be well if you spoke in signs as well as spoken words," said the old medicine man, as though he knew what thoughts were passing in Wolf's mind. "The white trader knows the sign language. Perhaps some of the White Chiefs may understand it. Anyhow, if you used signs with your words, Left-hand would be more careful," he added seriously.

"I will speak," said Wolf, wishing to please his friend.

"And for the peace?" asked Black-tongue, knowing the young man's temperament.

"Yes, for the peace," Wolf said simply.

"Good! We will move tomorrow instead of four days from now. The White Chiefs have asked for this change in our plans. A crier will tell the village about it this evening. We shall pitch our lodges near the mouth of the Judith tomorrow night. You will speak in the meeting with the Great White Chief after I have spoken. This has been arranged by the council. Ho!"

When Black-tongue left the lodge, Small-voice entered, beginning at once to arrange her household without mentioning Wolf's meeting with Breath-feather, moving silently so that she might not disturb her son, whose burning thoughts were of the girl and her fear of the half-breed. He knew that this fear was deep, that it was torturing her, or Breath-feather would not have spoken of it; nor would she have met him alone in his mother's lodge. Twice, without being conscious of stirring, he made room for his mother to spread robes before remembering that the village would move at daylight.

"Do not unpack too much, Mother," he said, as though awakening from sleep. "We are going to the Judith tomorrow."

"Black-tongue told you this?" she asked simply, beginning to pack again, without a word of complaint.

"Yes," he answered, returning to his thoughts of Breath-feather.

He realized that to ask Red-moccasin for the girl now, during his time of mourning for his brother, would be contrary to tribal custom. Besides this, even if Left-hand had not already spoken, his strange prophecy had so dazzled Red-moccasin that now, in the surge of the half-breed's sweeping popularity, might be the wrong time to ask for Breath-feather, since the ambitious war chief might be looking upon Left-hand as a prospective son-in-law. Nevertheless, even though Black-tongue might be right, and the half-breed's popularity might quickly wane, Wolf believed that if he would have Red-moccasin's daughter he must ask for her now, this day. He could, he *would*, forget custom for her. Even though the half-breed might have already spoken, Wolf determined to ask for Breath-feather as soon as he could find Red-moccasin. Without speaking a word of his intention to his mother, he went out to find the war chief.

Chapter 13

From the tops of tall lodges thin tails of blue smoke trailed upward to vanish in the clear air of the October afternoon. A drum was beating. Painted warriors with eagle-feather headdresses were dancing at the far edge of the village that would move so soon. A crowd had gathered round the dancers. About it bright-eyed children romped wildly, their happy voices sometimes drowning the deep tones of the drum.

There were no eavesdroppers about the White Chiefs' painted lodge now. Wolf saw that the lodge was unoccupied, that its door was open. Red-moccasin, with the visiting White Chiefs, would be watching the dancing. Hastening, Wolf began skirting the circle of the delighted spectators, so intent upon his errand that he would have passed Breath-feather without seeing her if she had not stepped backward from the edge of the crowd directly in front of him. "Try to see my mother every day," he whispered, pretending to look at the dancer's bobbing bonnets over the girl's head.

If she answered he did not hear her, and he could not have told her why he had delivered the message. Nevertheless, hurrying on, he was gladdened by having delivered it, attributing his sudden inspiration to his medicine, The Winds.

He found Red-moccasin with Left-hand and the white men inside the circle, a little apart from the other onlookers. Without hesitation, Wolf touched the arm of the war chief, beckoning him aside.

"This is neither a good time nor a good place to ask you for Breath-feather," he began, noting a quick look of embarrassment in Red-moccasin's eyes. "I have no horses to give you," he went on, determined to be perfectly understood, "but if you will give me your daughter, I will promise to tie ten good horses to your lodge before green grass comes again to the plains.

"You are a brave man, Wolf," said Red-moccasin, glancing uncomfortably to the group he had left. "I could feel proud of you as my son-in-law. But you have spoken too late. I have this day promised Breath-feather to Left-hand. He will take her soon after we have made the peace treaty at the mouth of the Judith."

Quick thoughts of his defeat, mingled with deep sorrow for Breath-feather, tightened Wolf's throat. "I could not properly have spoken sooner," he said evenly, turning away. He guessed that Left-hand knew exactly what had passed between Red-moccasin and himself. When a darting glance told him that the half-breed was smiling sarcastically, fierce, leaping anger paled his lips. He felt alone among his people. And as though a tribal epoch had been suddenly ended, the drum ceased its beating, the dancers and spectators dispersing in all directions.

Several times on his way to his mother's lodge Wolf talked gaily enough to young men who stopped him. Yes, he would speak at the peace meeting with the Great White Chief at the mouth of the Judith, he told them, not once permitting his inward turmoil to show itself in his eyes. He would keep his promise to Black-tongue. He would speak for the peace, even though he despised peace. He wished for war, unending battle.

He had scarcely seated himself in the lodge beside his father when the village crier began his round. "The village will move to the mouth of the Judith in the morning," he called, riding about the great circle of lodges. "We shall meet the Great White Chief there. We shall make peace with our enemies. Put away all your bad thoughts, all your hatreds, so that your hearts may be clean for the peace which our Chiefs will make with the others at the mouth of the Judith."

"Peace will be good," Wolf's father said, happily, as the crier's voice softened in distance. "You will speak at the meeting?" he asked his son.

"Yes, Father."

"And for the peace?" the man asked, a little anxiously, while filling his pipe.

"Yes, for the peace," Wolf answered, mechanically accepting the lighted pipe from his father, who, conscious of his son's preoccupation, left him to his thoughts.

"We have little left," Small-voice said gently, as she placed boiled meat before the two men. "I hope we shall find buffalo tomorrow."

"We will make an early start and kill some meat on our way to the Judith," Horned-bull promised, glancing at Wolf, who began slowly to eat as though he had not heard.

Long after the lodge fire had burned to dead ashes, Wolf lay upon his robe without sleeping. Thoughts of Breath-feather's life with Left-hand tormented him. The girl's fear of his cousin was so genuine that her union with the half-breed would be torture. This, and not his own loss, troubled Wolf most. He had long known that he wanted

Breath-feather, had known this from childhood. He had confidently expected to possess her. This had seemed to him to have been foreordained. Now he had lost her.

Perhaps if he had kept the horses which he had stolen from the Pecunnies, her father might have listened. He could then have given Red-moccasin ten, twenty, yes, fifty horses for his daughter. Now he had not even a single horse to ride. He was afoot. He smiled a little grimly at this thought, and then because it was the forerunner of approaching self-pity he put it out of his mind. His present poverty had not defeated him. Left-hand possessed no horses to give Red-moccasin. The half-breed had won Breath-feather by cunning chicanery. Could he be beaten? Could Breath-feather be saved from the half-breed? Would old Black-tongue help in this, or would his medicine, The Winds, point out a way?

Both Horned-bull and Small-voice heard Wolf go out of the lodge. Both knew that his mind was troubled, and yet, because they, and all of these simple plains people, were sincere individualists who believed that each life was governed by unseen powers, neither mentioned his going.

Outside on the wide plains beneath the stars Wolf sought guidance from the Night Winds that were gently ruffling the short grass. Slowly, and in turn, he fixed his eyes upon stars in the North, East, South, and West, softly chanting his invocation to the four Night Winds. And then, in humility, Wolf threw himself upon the plains, burying his face in the yellowed grass. Now his voice trembled with passion. "Oh, Winds, come to me! Speak to me! Lend me wisdom and strength! Lead me! I will follow! O Winds, I will follow!" he chanted over and over again until, nearly exhausted by the intensity of his pleading, he felt that his petition had been heard.

Reentering the lodge, he slept so soundly that he did not

hear his father go out to hunt buffalo on the way to the mouth of the Judith. Small-voice, moving quietly, packed her travois. Not until she took down the lodge skin, letting the light of the rising sun fall upon his face, did Wolf waken.

"Ho, Sleepy One," Small-voice smiled, giving him food. "Your father has gone to kill meat for us on the way to the Judith," she said, folding the lodge skin. "He is walking and leading his horse to save it for running buffalo. You can overtake him. But remember that we can pack only a little meat. I hope that the Great White Chief will give us some horses at the mouth of the Judith. Do you know about this, my Son?" she asked, finishing her packing.

"No, Mother," Wolf answered, slinging his quiver of arrows over his shoulder to follow his father. He saw that the village was moving, that already all the travois had gone, and that his mother's would be the last to leave. This, he knew, would annoy Small-voice. She had always found great satisfaction in being among the first to be ready to move. "I am sorry I slept so long," he said, as Small-voice started her horses, herself walking behind them on the sunlit plains.

"And, Mother," Wolf called, overtaking her, "I have asked Red-moccasin for Breath-feather. He has promised her to Left-hand. You may tell Breath-feather that I asked her father for her. Perhaps she already knows that her father has promised her to Left-hand. I have asked her to try to see you every day. I do not know why I asked this of her, Mother. But somehow I believe there will be a message for you to give her, that the Winds will help me, and that They told me to tell Breath-feather to see you every day."

Small-voice made no comment. As Wolf set out at a dog trot, turning a little northward, the course his father had most likely taken, she urged her horses forward in an effort to overtake the moving village. From a knoll, now far

100

off, she saw Wolf trotting among immense flocks of curlews that took wing, only to settle again when her son had
passed. They were getting ready to go away for the winter.
And yet they always returned to the plains. She wondered
if the curlews liked their winter country. Anyhow they always seemed so glad to get back to the plains that their
musical piping calls made her happy every springtime.
The curlews were late in gathering to go away this year.
This meant that the fall would be fine, the winter slow to
come to the plains.

Several large eagles were soaring over the curlews as
Small-voice descended the knoll. She saw one of the great
birds swoop to start the curlews flying so that he might
catch and kill one of them. Somehow, inured as she was to
the never-ending law, *kill or go hungry,* the swoop of the
eagle disturbed her. She became conscious of impending
strife, and yet, believing in her medicine-dream, she had
no fear for Wolf's life. Her son had told his father that he
would speak for peace at the mouth of the Judith. Why,
then, was she troubled, afraid of meeting the Great White
Chief?

Chapter 14

The Gros Ventres camped on the north bank of the Missouri, a little above the mouth of the Judith. Before sundown Small-voice had pitched her lodge in its rightful place in the village circle there and had arranged her household for a protracted stay. Horned-bull and Wolf had brought in all the buffalo meat that they and their horse could pack, so that the following days might be given wholly to the peacemaking.

Small-voice did not believe that Breath-feather should openly come to see her too often now that Red-moccasin had promised the girl to Left-hand. Nevertheless, she was determined to deliver to Breath-feather any message that Wolf might give her for transmission. Having no such message now, she was anxious to prevent the girl from coming needlessly to her lodge. The days were yet warm. A portion of the fresh buffalo meat had to be cut up and made ready for drying in tomorrow's sunlight. This gave Small-voice an opportunity to be out of doors, so that she could watch for Breath-feather, who, she knew, would come.

The western sky had reddened with a promise of a fair morrow when Small-voice, who had long been dallying with the meat, saw Breath-feather coming slowly toward her as though she, too, had misgivings about the propriety of her intended visit. Rising from her knees, Wolf's mother first looked searchingly in all directions. Then she said in signs: "Stop! Nothing now! See me tomorrow!"

"Yes!" The girl's right thumb and forefinger answered like a flash as she turned sharply to the left, asking admittance to a nearby lodge.

Far up and down the bank of the Missouri the smoke from many hundreds of buffalo-skin lodges crept upward to find the growing evening breeze and, meeting it, drifted lazily down the river like a thin, gray cloud. The Blackfeet had come; the three tribes of their nation were there. And now the Gros Ventres had pitched their lodges on the treaty ground, each tribe and each clan and each chief occupying hereditary positions in each separate village. The Crows, who had been invited, had not come. There was much talking about their absence. Village gossips who had already fraternized with their late enemies said that even now the Crows were hunting buffalo north of the Missouri, not two days' travel from the mouth of the Judith. Evidently this was to let the other tribes know that the Crows did not desire peace. "Good! Good!" said gossip. "Every man in every tribe that is here hates the Crows. A little war once in a while will be good for us. We will see that the Crows get all the fighting they need." However, the Flatheads had come from the west side of the Rockies. There were not many of them, only the head men of the tribe. And yet Victor, their renowned chief, had come to make a peace which would permit his tribesmen to hunt buffalo on the northern plains between the Yellowstone and Missouri rivers without having to fight for the privilege. Gossip said that already Victor was a favorite of Governor Stevens, the Great White Chief. Well, the Flatheads had always had to fight hard for their buffalo meat, and they were a small tribe. They would not need many buffalo, and there were millions of buffalo. Let the Flatheads have their needed buffalo meat and robes. Peace on the northern plains would be good for all the tribes. Besides the important bits of news, gossip had gathered other and meaner morsels. It said that two Pecunnie women had lately had their noses cut off because of infidelity to their men. This bit of scandal, spoken lightly by the Gros Ventre warriors, who had been visiting with their late enemies, quickly intrigued their women. They would be all eyes now. Formerly the Gros Ventres and Pecunnies had been close friends. Their villages had often been side by side until the war between the tribes had suddenly broken out. Perhaps the Gros Ventre women had known these mutilated Pecunnies or their mothers. Anyhow, they would soon see them, soon learn their names now.

Horned-bull, who had been among the Pecunnies and Bloods, brought all this and more to the lodge. He said that at the peace meeting James Bird, a half-breed, would interpret for the Blackfeet nation, that Bird and Left-hand and the Flathead chief, Victor, were constantly with the Great White Chief, that they ate together and walked together. "This peace will be good for us," he said, passing his pipe to Wolf, who had not left the lodge since he had first entered it.

But Wolf, who had quickly caught the delightful aroma of trade tobacco, which had been given his father in the Blood village, waved the pipe aside. Now, more than ever before, he was determined to obey the mandates of his medicine dream. "I will not smoke the White man's tobacco," he said without rancor. "The inner bark of the red willow and other barks and roots which grow here are good enough for me."

Wolf's life was his own, a part of the great enigma. Horned-bull found no fault with his son's determination, finishing the pipe alone. Small-voice, as though disturbed by Wolf's action, got up and went out of the lodge.

The October night was bright, the clear air keen enough to make one feel grateful for fire. Here, at the mouth of the Judith, on the endless plains of northern Montana, fires were burning in more than a thousand buffalo-skin lodges, their blurred lights weirdly marking the perfect circles of five villages. In all of them drums were beating. About bright fires built in the open men were dancing. Their sharp, exultant yelps were wild, like the yipping of coyotes. In the light of the Gros Ventre dance fire Small-voice saw the painted faces of Pecunnies and Flatheads, saw these tribesmen talking in the sign language, laughing merrily, with Gros Ventre warriors who yesterday would have gladly engaged them in battle.

The whole wonderful scene gripped her, held her fascinated, hope for permanent peace leaping in her heart; and yet, somehow, amid all this gaiety, Small-voice felt that there was tension, that over it all hatred and distrust had spread an imperceptible cloud. She well knew that red men seldom forgive and that they never forget. Even if peace should be made here, it would be like the dry grass of the plains. A single flash of flame would wipe it away.

Standing alone with her robe drawn tightly about her shoulders, watching the distant dancers and the lighted lodges, Small-voice saw the Great White Chief, Governor Stevens, join the onlookers at the Gros Ventre dance fire, his tall beaver hat and military coat trimmed with gold lace and red velvet making him a figure that she could never forget. With him were other white men and Bird and Lefthand. And now, inspired by the sight of her sister-in-law's son, her thoughts turned to Wolf and Breath-feather. Their plight seemed entirely hopeless. And yet Small-voice felt that somehow *The Ones Who Live Without Fire* would intervene. Wolf's life had been forecast in her medicine dream. It could not end here. For a moment, even though her love for her son was immeasurable, she wished that it might. When she reentered her lodge, the fire had burned out. Both Horned-bull and Wolf were sleeping. Lying down, she tucked her robe about her body, falling asleep with the rhythm of the beating drums in her ears.

The village crier awakened her at daylight. The peace would be made when the sun reached the middle of the sky. Both Horned-bull and Wolf sat up in their robes to listen to the message. "Peace will be good," said Horned-bull, getting up. "We must soon kill our winter's meat," he added, while Small-voice was kindling the lodge fire.

The morning sun, lighting the rolling plains and great river, lent the smoke from the lodge fires a bright blue, and in a single, widely spread film it lazed about the five villages as though loath to leave so peaceful a scene. Small-voice, going to the river for water, whispered her gratitude to the smoke for its augury of peace, reveling in the morning's beauty. As she dipped her kettle into the stream, a gunshot rang out. Instantly, in every village, scores of men leaped from lodges, their weapons in hand. Taking quick steps, calling anxious questions to each other, they learned that, while watering his horse, a thoughtless youth had fired at a skulking buffalo wolf. "Ahhhh!" they smiled, a little ashamed, going back into their lodges. Would these men make peace? *Could* they make peace? Smiling grimly, Small-voice prepared the morning meal.

This was to be a great day. Black-tongue, painted, bonneted, wearing his best shirt and leggings, called early upon Wolf, intent upon firing the young man for his coming speech. He understood why Wolf had not mingled with the crowd. His brother's death lay heavily upon him. Of all the young warriors of the tribe Wolf was most orthodox. "The young men will be eagerly listening for your voice," Black-tongue said seriously. "Speak strongly for peace, my Son!"

"I will speak," Wolf told him, dreading the ordeal.

"As soon as I have finished, you will speak," the old man reminded, following Horned-bull, now carefully attired, out of the lodge, where both men mounted beautifully caparisoned horses to ride in the joint procession. Round and round to the music of happy songs and the tinkling of thousands of hawk bells the warriors of the five tribes first paraded through each of the villages before settling down upon the chosen treaty ground.

Slowly, respectfully and afoot, the women and children followed, all wearing their choicest finery, all filled with excitement and hope for the peace. Now that the peace was actually to be made, there was scarcely a soul left in any of the villages.

Chapter 15

If, in the procession, there had been any intermingling, the tribes were now sharply segregated. Forming a great circle about the snapping ceremonial fire on the plains, the painted warriors seated themselves upon the ground, the feathers of their bonnets nodding in the midmorning breeze.

Wolf, who had walked to the scene, slipped quietly to a place immediately behind Black-tongue, sitting down with his back toward Breath-feather, who, unseen by him, was standing with her mother on the outskirts of the crowd of Gros Ventre women.

The girl was conscious of a satisfied stirring among the young warriors upon her lover's arrival. She saw that his face was painted, that his fine head was bare, and that his shirt and leggings, the handiwork of his mother, were strikingly handsome. If only she could see his eyes. She knew that they would be piercingly eager, that they could never hide a lie; and Wolf had told Black-tongue that he was for the peace. She fixed her own eyes upon his head now, wondering if he would feel her presence.

Black-tongue turned, greeting Wolf warmly. "After to-day we can hunt buffalo wherever we choose, without having to fight," he was saying, when Governor Isaac Stevens, wearing his tall hat and gaudy coat, appeared beside the fire. With him were two other white men, carrying papers, a stool, and a small table, which they placed a little way from the fire. Following these, as though burdened with their importance, were the interpreters for the tribes, a short, bowlegged half-breed with bobbed hair and rings in his ears, James Bird, and Left-hand, resplendent in a scarlet shirt.

Governor Stevens himself hoisted an American flag to the top of a pole which had been prepared, removed his tall hat, reverently saluting the banner of his country, thus deeply impressing the Indians. Of all audiences on earth none can be more courteous or respectful than a gathering of red men, so that when Governor Stevens held up his hand, the silence of these wild hunters made him marvel. Even the little children were so still that he could hear the gently moving water of the Missouri when he began to speak.

"I know that you wish to hunt buffalo for winter meat and that you will leave this treaty place this afternoon, the Flatheads going first because they must cross the mountains," he began.

Then he told the Indians that he had traveled far to help them make a peace that would last and be good for all. He said that if this peace were made he would distribute many presents which the Great White Father in Washington had sent them. He told the Indians that breaking the peace, if it were made, would bring trouble to the breaker, because the Great White Father would help in punishing the peace breaker. He dwelt long on the blessings of peace and in glowing words expressed his delight in seeing so many tribesmen there and spoke highly of their decorum, finishing with a restated promise of punishment of peace breakers.

The governor's speech, constantly interrupted to give the interpreters opportunity to transmit the words to the various tribes, required much time, the patient red men listening intently to the end.

The leading chiefs of the Blackfeet Nation, Pecunnies, Bloods, and Blackfeet, followed, each readily agreeing to the peace. Victor, of the Flatheads, stirred his audience so deeply that when he had finished Governor Stevens shook the chief's hand. Ten speeches had been made when Blacktongue stepped forward to speak for the Gros Ventres, his seamed face a picture of power. In a moment he had the tribes laughing at their own folly. By the cunning use of homely similes the old man reached their hearts as no other man had reached them. "We have young warriors among us. Let Wolf, our youngest Chief, speak his mind," he ended, bowing his thanks to Governor Stevens and the interpreters.

Wolf, who had carried no robe, stepped lightly forward to the circle's center, his piercing eyes sweeping the hundreds of faces in an impersonal glance. Until now, having given all his attention to the speeches, he had not looked upon them. Fascinated by the power and splendor of so many strong men whose eyes were upon him, he was unable to find the words which he had chosen until a gust of Wind brushed his neck. "Yes," he whispered, now sure of himself. Then, walking away from his people, facing first one tribe and then another, he began to speak eloquently, accompanying his spoken words with carefully made signs. These, he knew, would be understood even though Left-hand lied.

"I have listened carefully to the words of the Chiefs, all older and wiser men than I am," he began, speaking slowly, his resonent voice carrying to the ears of all. "When much snow has fallen upon the plains, hiding everything

110

there beneath a white robe, a few flakes of additional snow cannot make the plains whiter."

Men in every tribe nodded approval, listening anxiously for this young man's words. But suddenly Wolf ceased speaking. Striding across the wide circle, his eyes blazing, he stopped before a warrior of the Flatheads who had only one eye. "Ho!" he cried, his right arm shooting out, his rigid finger pointing, the fine muscles of his lithe body tense as steel. "Ho! Flathead, coward!" he taunted, bending nearer. "You copy Pecunnies in dressing your hair. You fooled me that day. Does any man here believe that I will make peace with *you*, the man who killed my brother. No, Dog-face, never!" he panted, striking the Flathead's cheek a resounding slap with the flat of his hand.

Even though Wolf's words were unintelligible, the one-eyed warrior perfectly understood the blow. Leaping to his feet, knife in hand, the Flathead struck viciously at Wolf, who nimbly avoided the weapon.

"Ho!" cried the boy, drawing his own knife from its scabbard, "You will fight, Flathead, Dog-face?" he sneered, crouching to close with the tall warrior, who had already stabbed thrice, narrowly missing him.

Shocked, breathless, the circle of peacemakers rose as one man, hesitating to move farther, even a hand. Weapons had been left in the lodges. Was this conspiracy some cunning trick of the white men to catch them all unarmed with only knives at their belts?

"Ahhh!" A quick sign of deep relief ran round the wide circle when suddenly, from behind, Black-tongue and Chief Victor threw their arms about the bodies of the fighting pair, drawing them apart.

The one-eyed Flathead, harshly denounced by Chief Victor, sat down sulkily, his one eye burning with hatred. Wolf, feeling a cool breeze press his back, stalked across the circle, going alone to the nearly empty Gros Ventre village, feeling that many men, both friends and foes, had not, in their hearts, condemned him.

The prompt action of Black-tongue and Victor narrowly saved the treaty. Governor Stevens warmly shook their hands and then, standing with his arms about their shoulders, spoke feelingly in praise of their help for peace.

Breath-feather, her heart racing from excitement caused by Wolf's boldness among so many older men, saw her lover go alone to the village. She was determined to see him, somehow, to tell him that her father had promised her to Left-hand; and yet no excuse would permit her to follow Wolf to the village. He loved her. Could he save her from the half-breed, she wondered; or, she shuddered at the thought, must she, by death, save herself?

"See! See, they are making the peace!" Her mother's voice aroused her when Black-tongue, Red-moccasin, and the chiefs of all the assembled tribes touched the pen in Governor Stevens's hand, thus ratifying the treaty.

Men were laughing, joking, as they turned away. "Now for the big hunt," they said happily to each other, leaving the treaty ground to drive in their horses. Merry women and children, carrying the presents, bright-colored calicos and useless trinkets, hastened to their villages to pack up, ready for moving, all anxious to be out on the plains after the buffalo.

By the time Breath-feather and her mother had reached their lodge, the Flatheads had already crossed the Missouri, heading away toward the distant Rockies with the good news of the peace treaty for their waiting tribesmen. But now a crier told the assembled Gros Ventres that the tribe would not move to the plains until morning. Relieved by this sudden change of plan, Breath-feather hoped to meet Wolf, or at least to see his mother. Taking a kettle, she went to the river for water, her eyes searching the circle of lodges for Wolf or Small-voice. Neither was in sight. Nevertheless, Small-voice had been watching the door of Red-moccasin's lodge from her own. Now, with two kettles, she followed Breath-feather to the river.

Without the loss of a moment Small-voice, stopping near the girl, told her that Wolf had asked her father for her, that his suit had been rejected in favor of Left-hand. "Wolf has gone," she whispered, pretending to draw a design in the mud on the river's bank so that any watcher would be deceived. "He has taken a rope and a robe, filled his quiver with arrows, and gone. I do not know where. He told me to tell you that if this evening you see excitement in the village, if you see men gather, hear them speaking of him, you are to go to the point on the river below the treaty ground after dark. Wolf will be waiting for you there. If you want my son, go. But first, try to come to my lodge. Ho!"

Before the frightened girl had had time to understand the message, Wolf's mother had filled her kettles and gone. Trembling, cold with sudden fear, Breath-feather dipped her own kettle into the water, her thoughts whirling dizzily. She could never afterward remember her return to the lodge, nor any spoken word by man or woman, until a crier began calling the warriors to assemble. Now, aroused by the tread of running men, she hastily drew a robe about her shoulders and went outside.

Men were gathering round two riders on panting horses. Breath-feather saw that one of the riders was Victor, the Flathead Chief. The other was his bow-legged interpreter. She saw Victor dismount, beckoning Governor Stevens, who was already running toward the gathering. In the growing dusk the girl heard Victor speak to the governor rapidly, forcefully at the end handing the White man an arrow, the bow-legged one translating the chief's words into English. And now, wondering, she saw the governor hastily embrace Victor, saw him give the Flathead chief two fine horses and his tall hat and military coat.[1] But not until Left-hand turned Governor Stevens's speech into Gros Ventre did Breath-feather understand a spoken word.

Somebody had killed the one-eyed Flathead, scalped him, and stolen his horse. Victor, who knew that the shaft which he, himself, had found in the dead man's breast was a Gros Ventre arrow, had brought the condemning bolt to the village. The arrow was passing from man to man. Breath-feather, peeping between the shoulders of two warriors, saw the arrow coming, saw it stop for a moment before her, saw the men nod their heads, "Ahhh," they said, readily, "this is Wolf's arrow."[2]

Even as Governor Stevens and the now thoroughly placated Flathead chief began to talk to her father and Left-hand, Breath-feather ran to the lodge of Wolf's mother. "What shall I do?" she whispered, her voice trembling, her eyes not upon the woman but upon the darkening doorway.

Small-voice took Breath-feather in her arms. "As you think best, my Daughter," she whispered, lovingly brushing the girl's beautiful hair with her fingers. "If you want my son, you must go. He will be waiting," she went on, remembering that the moments were precious. "And if you go, take this with you," she said, giving Breath-feather a light pack neatly wrapped in a buffalo robe.

Taking the pack, she had a moment of fleeting and fortunate indecision. Somebody on horseback was nearing the lodge. Breathlessly the two women listened until the rider had passed. Then, pressing her dry lips against the cheek

[1] The author saw the hat and coat among the Flatheads in the summer of 1935.—F. B. L.
[2] Arrows were marked.—F. B. L.

114

of Wolf's mother, the girl dropped the lodge door behind her, fleeing into the shadows.

Crossing the treaty ground, dodging the unshadowed spots, she headed downstream toward a timbered point that jutted out, turning the river, the pack beneath her arm. Would Wolf be there? Could she find him? What would happen to her if Wolf had failed to reach the point? She would never go back to the village now. The women would spurn her, call her a prostitute. If Wolf did not meet her at the point, she would go on and on until she died.

A rocky bar, its stones round and smooth, stretched from the river's cutbank to the point. Here there was no cover, no shadow. Leaping from bank to the bar, Breath-feather heard a horse whinny in the darkness across the river. "Wolf! Wolf!" she called, stumbling over the slippery stones.

"Yes, yes, Breath-feather, my heart-woman. I am here." Wolf's arms were about her, drawing her to his breast. "Do not tremble," he whispered, passionately kissing her. "You are safe now. You are safe."

For moments, which Wolf knew were dangerous, he held the fondly nestling girl, kissing her lips, her eyes, her hair, the only sound the gently moving water of the great river.

Then, tenderly lifting her face so that he might look into her eyes, he whispered, "I will not take you until you know that I have today made myself an outlaw and that if you go with me you, too, will be an outlaw. And yet, I promise that if you do go with me, I will never have another woman."

"Yes, Wolf, I know; oh, I know," she sighed, brushing a lock of hair from his forehead. "I heard the message. I saw your arrow. Go! Go, quickly, Wolf," she whispered, with a swift glance at the circle of firelit lodges. "I will follow."

"We have spoken," he said reverently, leading the girl beyond the point to a tiny raft of dry drift logs. Drawing the bobbing craft to him, he placed his foot firmly upon the rope that held it. "Undress," he whispered, stripping himself bare. Then, folding Breath-feather's clothes with his own, he placed them with the pack upon the raft, wading into the deep, icy water, with the naked girl following. In a moment they were swimming, the current of the wide river slowly sweeping them downstream, their heads and the raft towed by Wolf, scarcely discernible on the dark water.

At last, dripping and embarrassed, Breath-feather sought the dark shadows of an overhanging bank while Wolf pulled the raft to the river's southern shore, nearly opposite the mouth of Birch Creek. Handing the girl her clothes, he stole a single, lingering glance at her naked beauty and then, tossing his own apparel to the bank, hastily rescued the rawhide rope from the raft, letting the short logs drift away.

Dressed, Wolf slung his quiver of arrows across his shoulder, leading Breath-feather through a dark grove of giant cottonwoods to a saddled horse tied at the edging plains. Securing the girl's pack to the cantle, he deftly arranged his own robe across the saddle's seat, holding her in his arms a moment before bidding her to mount.

Now, as shadows move, Wolf led the way down the Missouri. Walking rapidly, keeping always within the friendly tree shadows of the skirting groves, his heart singing with every backward glance at the following girl, Wolf devoutly whispered his gratitude to The Winds.

116

Chapter 16

As she glowed with the reaction which the swift walk had given her young blood after swimming in the icy water, Breath-feather's first thoughts were of her mother.

Polygamy was necessary to her people. Constant warfare had so reduced the men that the women outnumbered them, sometimes four to one. Like many leading men of the Gros Ventres, Breath-feather's father possessed four wives, all of them sisters. The three older ones had always been jealous of Breath-feather's mother, who was comparatively young. The rule of priority permitted conspiracy, so that the three had so overburdened their younger sister that she was already breaking down. Breath-feather's father had never so much as mentioned the unfair division of work in his household, though he must have noticed it. Like most of his tribesmen, Red-moccasin looked lightly upon the affairs of women. "Let women settle their own controversies," was his motto, and this was general among the men of the plains.

Breath-feather knew that by now her mother would be searching for her, calling at the lodges of friends, questioning, wondering. And yet the girl believed that when her mother learned the truth she would not condemn her, that, remembering her own life with her older sisters, she would be secretly glad her daughter had escaped such a life. Wolf had promised that he would never have another woman, and notwithstanding custom, Breath-feather believed her lover.

Oh, her father would be furious! If he and his clan should find them now, tonight, they might take Wolf's life. Tomorrow? Tomorrow, even though he had not paid for her with horses, she would be Wolf's woman. And what could her father do about it? Wolf would yet pay for her. Had he not already given the tribe many horses? Even now her father's horses had been given him by Wolf, who because of his generosity was now afoot, walking ahead of her, leading her where? She did not know. She did not care.

A quick thought of Left-hand chilled her. For an instant her fear of the half-breed returned. He would talk now, talk to everybody, telling lies. Oh, if only he would dare to follow them now, tonight! Wolf would kill him, kill him as he would kill a skunk. Anyhow, Wolf had saved her from Left-hand. Nevertheless, the women would talk, and they would never, never forget. How she hated the thought of women whispering about her in her mother's presence. But the men would smile, tolerantly. After all, she was only a woman, and women were made for men. "There are too many women," the men would say. "Why quarrel with a man who steals a woman?"

And this same thought was in Wolf's mind now. He had stolen a woman. His tribesmen would look upon him as a common thief until he paid plentifully for Breath-feather. He would pay for her, pay promptly, handsomely. Even now, running away with Red-moccasin's daughter, he was looking for the Crows. He knew that they were hunting buffalo north of the Missouri. He would find them, steal some of their horses, and give them to Breath-feather's father. He might have more easily stolen horses from the

118

Pecunnies. But this would again bring war to his people. He loved his tribesmen. Neither the Crows nor the Sioux had made peace with the Gros Ventres, so that he had a right to steal horses from either of these tribes. He knew that if he stole horses from the Crows the theft would be charged to either his own tribe or the Pecunnies. He could see no harm in this. Anyhow, he himself had made no peace with any tribe, anybody. He had not even spoken for the peace. The Winds, barely in time, had stopped his speech, or he would have committed himself to peace with the Flatheads and Pecunnies. Now, thanks to The Winds, he was free, his own master. And with the help of The Winds, he would continue to be his own master. He had Breath-feather, his heart-woman. He would keep her, care for her, love her as no other man had ever loved a woman.

He knew that his mother had always expected him to have Breath-feather, that she loved the girl and had secretly helped her escape from the village. What a good, brave mother she was, gently dominating his father, who had taken no other woman. Would Red-moccasin suspect his mother of having conspired with Breath-feather? No. Wolf felt certain that his mother was too clever to be apprehended by the war chief. His father, knowing nothing, could tell nothing. How old Black-tongue would smile, chuckling over this defeat of Left-hand. Wolf wondered why the old man had not dared to denounce Left-hand. If Black-tongue would only tell how he knew that Left-hand had lied about counting coup on the Pecunnie at the Teton crossing, he, Wolf, would denounce the half-breed, not casually, but in open council, and he would defy Left-hand. But would he, Wolf, have a seat in the tribal council now? This was a troubling thought. Treason was punishable by death. Had he, in killing the one-eyed Flathead, committed treason, the Flatheads having signed the peace with the

Gros Ventres? He wondered and, wondering, walked faster, the horse bearing Breath-feather trotting behind him.

The *Little Grey*, the false dawn, was in the sky when Wolf, with a whispered prayer to the Winds, stopped in a tiny meadow hidden by trees and bushes beside the Missouri. Unsaddling, he led the horse to water and then, having staked the animal on the choicest available grass, went again to the river, this time to swim before breaking his fast. Breath-feather, unwrapping the pack which Small-voice had given her, smiled happily over the pemmican, dried berries, moccasins, flint and steel, sinew, needles, an awl, and an extra rawhide rope, many little necessities which Wolf's mother had gathered for the runaways.

"See, Wolf! See, we are *rich*," she whispered merrily, her pretty head lifted, her lips inviting.

"Yes," he answered, eagerly reaching for her, "you are rich in having a good mother-in-law, and I am rich in having you, my heart-woman."

They were not hurried now. There were no accusing eyes in their new world. The sky was brightening in the east when they had eaten of the pemmican. Then, after Wolf had brought her a drink of water in a horn cup, Breath-feather made their bed, spreading the soft robes beneath the yellow leaves of overhanging cottonwoods to nestle in Wolf's arms.

Lovers, even before either had known the craving of passionate desire, neither noticed the progress of the sun. The bright day grew, its dazzling sunlight offering entrancing glimpses of the calm river through clusters of golden leaves, and yet Wolf and Breath-feather saw only each other. Once when two chickadees lit upon a leafy bough overhanging their robes, Breath-feather sat up, her slender finger pointing at the tiny birds. "Ho!" she said, in mimic scorn, "you two have been spying! And you have been listening! Shame! You chickadee-people are always spying, always listening," she scolded severely, shaking her finger. "Go away, you two who are wearing *Old-man*'s [1] necklace. Go away, and don't you dare to tell," she warned, pretending to strike at the friendly little birds.

Wolf forgot the fatigue of the night, forgot danger, forgot even his mission. So entranced was he by Breath-feather's witchery and his own fondness that he gave no thought to his situation until the sun was in the south. Then, folding his woman in his arms, he slept, her breath sweet in his nostrils. No sounds disturbed the sleepers. Not even a coyote crossed the tiny meadow where the satisfied horse lazily cropped the grass.

The sun was setting, the tree shadows long when Wolf awakened, sitting up to look fondly at his sleeping woman. Her arm, bare to the elbow, was outside the covering, the slender fingers of her hand partially hidden in the robe's fur, one long braid of her black hair lying across her half-naked breast. Feeling his eyes, even in her sleep, Breath-feather stirred, pulling up the robe. How he loved her, his heart-woman!

Slipping quietly from the bed, he went first to the river, looking, listening, before refreshing himself in the water. Then, when he had let the horse drink, he climbed a cottonwood so that he might look at the plains beyond the river. A band of antelope was near the stream, some of the animals lying down. Beyond, in the clear evening air, he saw a great herd of buffalo. They, too, were grazing. They had not been disturbed by the Crows. If the Crow hunters were killing buffalo north of the Missouri, they must be farther down the stream. He would have to go on.

Hoping to dissuade him, Breath-feather proposed that

[1] The Creator, and yet not the Almighty Power.—F. B. L.

121

they go to the Pecunnies, now that these tribesmen had signed the peace. "Our tribes used to live together, hunt together, and make war together," she said. "We, you and I, know many Pecunnies," she went on, reminding him that often men and women sought refuge with alien tribes. "We have a Cree and his woman, and a Lakota with his woman in our village even now," she finished, hoping that they might turn back up the river.

But Wolf was determined. "Would you have me pay your father for you?" he asked, kissing her lips. "Would you?" he pressed.

"Yes, Wolf," she sighed. "And yet I am afraid, afraid for you, Wolf. One hand against so many men——"

"Ho!" he interrupted. "Alone! That is the way to steal horses. Do not be frightened. Come!"

She was an Indian woman. Wolf was her man now, and Wolf would have his way. A young moon, too young to light the coming night, was hanging in the western sky, the frosty air crisp with warnings of approaching winter when she mounted the horse to ride in darkness down the river, Wolf walking ahead.

Twice they passed antelope that bounded away to lose themselves on the plains. Near midnight a grizzly bear, traveling up the river toward the Rockies, so frightened Breath-feather's horse that he swerved sharply, nearly throwing her; but there was no stopping, no pause. Wolf, striding ahead, his eyes and ears keened by expectation, cut across bends in the river without once slackening his pace. The young moon, scarcely waiting for dusk, had long ago left the sky to the stars. Breath-feather thought that never before had she seen them so bright, *The Wolf's Trail*, the Milky Way, so unbrokenly long. Now and then, when near the river, she could hear the water washing over gravelly bars. No breeze was stirring. "The Winds must be sleeping," she thought, as Wolf, rounding the base of a high knoll that nearly reached the river, turned southward to cut across a bend.

Following, her horse now walking, now trotting to keep Wolf's shadowy form in sight, Breath-feather felt the touch of a breeze as she rounded the knoll. Instantly her head lifted, her nostrils working eagerly, her body tensing. Then, drumming her moccasined heels against the horse's sides, she urged him forward.

"Hisssst! Hisssst! Wolf!" she whispered in the knoll's shadow. "I smell smoke."

Stopping as though he had met an arrow, Wolf turned his face in all directions, his hand upon Breath-feather's knee. The breeze had passed. The keen night air was still, without an odor excepting that of sage.

"Yes, yes. I smelled smoke, Wolf," she insisted, knowing that he was not convinced. "It was *old* smoke, smoke from a dying lodge fire, that the Little Winds brought to me," she told him, her nose again busy.

"*Now!*" she whispered, suddenly leaning forward. "Do you smell it, Wolf?"

"Yes," he said, kissing her hand. "You were higher from the ground than I. The Winds, in their search for me, found *you;* and they *told* you, my heart-woman," he explained, his faith in his medicine firmer than ever.

He dared go no farther. He must learn the source of the smoke. If it had come from Crow lodges, he must know their location before going on. All night he had noted hiding places as he passed them. Now, turning the horse, he led it back up the river to a thick grove surrounded by bushes. Here, after loosening the saddle's cinch, he let the hungry horse graze upon whatever grass it could find, holding its tethering rope in his hand. They could hear the river and the movements of the patient horse, and yet in the dark grove they could see nothing excepting small patches of the starry sky above the tall trees. Settling down with their backs against a cottonwood, Wolf and Breath-feather drew their robes tightly about their shoulders to wait for daylight. As though bewildered, the vagrant breezes came to them from all directions, sometimes bringing faint scents of smoke. Twice, after prolonged whisperings, Wolf, lifting his robe, covered both Breath-feather's head and his own beneath it, fondling the snuggling girl, kissing her again and again.

Chapter 17

At dawn Wolf was in a treetop. Beneath him, where Breath-feather waited, the fallen leaves were white with frost, and more leaves were falling. Each time he moved in the tree, a shower of yellowed leaves fluttered to the frosty ground. No buffalo were in sight, no antelope. The plains, curtained by a purple mist, were bare, lifeless, waiting for the sun. Suddenly in the mist downstream Wolf saw a lance of smoke dart upward, then another, and yet another, until they numbered ten. The Crow village of ten lodges was in sight! Wolf wished there were more lodges. So small a village here, so near the Gros Ventres and Pecunnies, would be especially watchful. Even though he had spoken lightly of them to Breath-feather, Wolf knew that the Crows were capable men.

Now, as the sun came, like dark specks on the plains, Wolf saw the Crows' horses, more than a hundred, perhaps nearly two hundred, head. They were a little way up the stream from the village. Carefully noting the knolls where in the night the herders might sit, he fixed the whole scene in his mind, planning his night's work as carefully as a commanding general plans a coming battle.

The frost crystals on the dry leaves were sparkling about Breath-feather's moccasins when Wolf descended the tree, happy as a little child. Seizing her, he led the girl in the steps of the *Owl-dance,* chanting the air, his voice growing stronger as his spirit rose.

"Shhh! Not so loud," she cautioned, breaking away, her fingers upon her lips, her eyes merry nevertheless.

"Ho!" he laughed, taking her into his arms. "The Crows are just now waking up and are far away. Heyah, hoyo—heyah!" he sang, dancing about the now-smiling girl.

"Come, let us steal out to the river. Let us then eat before we hide for the day," he said, playful as a puppy.

Finding a secluded place where the horse might satisfy its hunger, Wolf staked the animal while Breath-feather made their bed. She knew that the day would be long and that Wolf would be restless. Besides, she dreaded the coming night. And yet so cheerful, so attentive was Wolf that she felt surprise when the sunlight began to wane, the air to grow crisper among the shadowing cottonwoods. Twice after the sun had turned westward Wolf had climbed a tree, even though he knew that when night finally came he must wait until the young moon was down before setting forth.

"We must cross the river as soon as darkness comes," he told Breath-feather after his last survey of the Crow village. "I have seen a good place for you to wait for me, a place where you will be safe and comfortable. The Winds have spoken," he said, with deep assurance. "We shall be lucky tonight."

Wolf did not wait for the moon to set before crossing the river, Breath-feather naked upon the horse, himself towing a raft bearing their clothes, his bow and quiver, and the pack. As he had planned, they landed where a cutbank had long ago slid into the river, forming an incline from the water to the plains. Several young cottonwoods were growing on the incline, with scattered thickets of bushes;

and immediately at its top, as though fashioned for this enterprise, the incline was flattened so that for twenty feet there was level ground sheltered by the young cottonwoods. Better than this, in caving from the bank the incline had left the edge of the plains cut straight down nearly three feet, forming a perfect breastwork which would hide Breath-feather and, if tied lower down the incline, even the horse.

So impatient was Wolf that as soon as he had attended to Breath-feather's comfort, notwithstanding that the moon was yet in the sky, he prepared to set out. He had eaten nothing since the afternoon and would eat nothing now. "Only a fool fills his belly when his head must do more work than his back," he laughed, winding a rawhide rope about his waist. Then, picking up his dressed wolf skin, he took his woman in his arms. "I will be careful," he promised.

"Keep the horse saddled and ready," he told her now. "Let your ears be open. If you hear horses coming, you will know that I am behind them, close behind them. Be sure to wait until the horses pass you here. Then ride out behind them. But," he kissed her playfully, "if you first hear guns, and *then* horses, you will know that I am *ahead* of the horses, and that I am traveling fast. If this should happen, you must keep hidden until you can ride back up the river. You must travel only at night, hiding daytimes until I overtake you."

"But if you do not come, if——"

"Ho!" he stopped her, laughing at her fears. "The Crows will be feasting. Their bellies will be full. I will come, and I shall bring horses to give to your father. Do not feel afraid, my heart-woman."

She held him, tearfully pleading that he give up his venture, thoughts of her own plight if he did not return chilling her heart. But he would not listen. "The Winds have spoken. They have never failed to help me," he told her, gently freeing himself from her arms.

"Remember my words," he cautioned, setting out. And then, turning back, he said seriously, "If I do not overtake you, find our people. Go to my mother's lodge. She will make you welcome until I come. Ho!"

He was gone. The frightened girl, sobbing, hid her face in her robe. All her life she had known that the women of her tribe, and of all the tribes of the plains, often faced such moments as these; and yet, not until the moon was down, not until the stars had grown glitteringly bright in the sky could she find scorn for her fears. Wolf loved her. Wolf was brave. He had powerful Helpers. Wolf would return to her.

Lifting her face from her robe, she was quick to feel Wind in her hair, a Wind that blew down the river toward the Crow lodges. "Ah," she sighed, ashamed of her weakness, "you have been waiting to tell me that you are with him. Forgive me, O Winds, I am a woman." Then, the chill Wind drying her tears, she whispered, praying fervently, "Oh, help him. Help Wolf tonight. Send him back to me, O Winds. Wolf is my man. I love him."

She felt suddenly light, lifted above danger and, with new and firmer faith in Wolf's Helpers, leaned her arms upon the edge of the plains to look toward the distant Crow village. It was not in sight from the incline. Climbing upon the plains, she saw the lodges, ten dim dots of light that held her fascinated. She was sure that besides the lights in the lodges she saw a fire in the Crow village. Perhaps the Crows *were* feasting! If only their bellies were full as Wolf had said they would be! And yet she knew that there would be guards with the horses. Would the bellies of these men be full enough to dull their wits?

She looked anxiously at the sky. The night was young. Wolf could not yet have reached the Crow horses. Even if he had reached them, he would have to work carefully, slowly. He could scarcely reach her before midnight. How often she had listened to stories of horse stealing! Now she was out on a raid herself, out with her man to steal horses. She would help all she could. Wolf would be hungry. She would have some pemmican ready in her hand when she rode out behind the stolen horses. She would ride her horse to Wolf and immediately hand him the pemmican. Then she would ride as she had never ridden, driving the horses up the river with her man. She would eat a little pemmican now herself, and she would tighten the saddle's cinch, see to the pack, get ready for Wolf's coming. Oh, how she would ride when Wolf came!

Near midnight, even though she struggled to hold her spirits high, fear again tormented her. The Wind had died. Not a breath of air was stirring now. Had The Winds forgotten Wolf, she dared to wonder, climbing the cut bank once more to stare steadily into space, its emptiness stabbing her eyes. The lights of the Crow lodges were gone. Only the open fire burned in the village.

"O Winds," she whispered, her fear growing, "help him, help him." And she believed that her supplication had been answered when the Wind, rising near midnight, touched her face. "Ahh," she sighed, her fear dying as she recognized the Wind's direction, "you have awakened. You are helping Wolf, my man. Forgive me, O Winds."

Even though it had dispelled her sharper fears, if Breathfeather could have seen Wolf when the rising Wind began to stir the plains' grass, she would have been terrified. Wearing the wolfskin upon his back, its head covering the back of his own, its ears erect, Wolf had crept toward the Crow horses, his every action simulating a prowling wolf.

The Crow horses, grazing in separated bands containing from twenty to thirty head, were not far from the base of a high knoll. Upon this knoll Wolf expected to find the night herder. Small patches of sagebrush offered perfect cover. In these patches Wolf had no fear of detection. But the patches were small, scattered, often far apart. To reach the nearest band of horses he would have to cross a wide space devoid of cover. Besides this the starlight was bright, so bright that there were shadows beside the bunches of sage. He wondered why he could not see the Crow herder on the knoll. He must locate this man, know his position exactly, before crossing the open space.

Creeping forward, his bow and two arrows in his left hand, Wolf stopped at the edge of the dangerous ground. He could hear the voices of men about a fire in the Crow village, see men in the firelight. He knew that they were feasting on fat buffalo meat. And yet try as he might he could see no herder on the high knoll. The Winds were still; no breath of air was stirring. The night was growing older. He must hurry. Between himself and the high knoll, a third of the way across the open space, the shadow of a smaller knoll lay upon the plains. If he could reach this shadow and keeping within it creep around the knoll's base, he might discover the herder on the higher knoll.

Knowing that Breath-feather would be anxious, Wolf did not hesitate now. Carefully readjusting the wolfskin for the dangerous venture, he moved forward, creeping slowly toward the knoll shadow, his muscles tensed, his eyes straining at its blackness. He had reached the shadow's edge, was creeping into it when, like a restraining hand, the Night Wind pressed his cheek, stopping him as though he had been stunned by a blow.

The wolfskin had slipped forward, its nose hanging near Wolf's eyes. He dared not lift a hand to raise it. Instead he lifted his head to see higher, his first glance nearly freezing his blood. A man, the Crow herder, not five bow lengths ahead, was staring at him from the shadow.

A quick surge of fear swept Wolf's body, the Crow herder, so suddenly and so dangerously near, seeming to fasten his hands and knees to the ground. He dared not move, dared not even turn his eyes from the man's face until voices from the Crow village reached his ears. Now, his blood warming a little, Wolf saw that the Crow's chin rested upon his breast, that the man was asleep. Smiling contemptuously, Wolf rose to his knees, fitting the notch of an arrow to his bowstring, and only The Winds saved the herder's life.

"Yes," Wolf whispered obediently to his Helpers, beginning carefully to work a band of twenty horses farther and farther away from the knolls, creeping back and forth behind them until the horses stopped to drink from a sluggish creek that flowed into the nearby Missouri. Here was Wolf's opportunity. Unwinding the rope from his waist, he caught a young stallion, putting two half hitches on the horse's underjaw. And yet he did not mount, continuing to drive the horses up the river until he knew that the sound of pounding hoofs could not reach either the sleeping herder or the Crow village. Then, mounting the stallion, Wolf urged the horses to a trot. He would let them get their wind before making them run.

Chapter 18

Breath-feather, quick to catch the first sounds of traveling horses, leaned eagerly forward a moment, her heart leaping. Yes, horses were coming! They were trotting. Wolf was coming! Belting her robe so that it would be tight about her waist, the happy girl jumped down from the plains to the incline, running to her horse, untying it, ready to mount.

Excited by her swift movements, the horse was restless, anxious to be gone, nearly getting away from her. Speaking evenly, softly, she quieted the animal; but when she saw the horse's ears prick eagerly forward at the sound of the coming ponies, she feared that it might whinny, frightening the coming band, swerving it, making trouble for Wolf. Tucking the pemmican which she had kept for her man into the folds of her robe, she placed her hand over the horse's muzzle, her fingers ready to smother a whinny by pressing the nostrils together. The Winds were with Wolf. The oncoming horses would not smell her, would not take fright until they had passed her. Holding tightly to her nervous horse, scarcely breathing, the muscles of her young body taut as bowstrings, Breath-feather waited until the stolen horses had passed her hiding place.

Then, with a glad cry like that of a night bird, she mounted, dashing up the cutbank behind them, her sudden appearance making them run. Frantically digging her heels against her mount's sides Breath-feather dropped the end of her rope to the ground, sending it snapping at the nearest Crow horse, her spirits shooting up to the stars at the speed which her rope's end gave the horses. For a moment, in her happy excitement she forgot even the pemmican in her robe. Now, guiding her horse to Wolf's side, she handed him the meat. "You must be hungry," she said, her horse running beside Wolf's.

Leaning, Wolf kissed her, for a moment holding her to him. "I was long in coming," he whispered, understanding her anxiety. "The Winds were sleeping. I had to wait," he explained, letting her go.

"Yes, Wolf, I know. I knew when they awakened," she told him, wondering if he could ever know the torture of fear.

"Not so fast," Wolf cautioned her, as she lashed again at the stolen horses with her rope. "We have far to go. We must save their strength for needed speed. The sun may bring the Crows."

On and on, seeing only skulking wolves on the plains, they rode toward the distant mountains, all the horses on a swinging lope until the stars faded in the light of the rising sun. Then, leaving Breath-feather to keep the Crow horses going, Wolf climbed to a knoll top, looking anxiously eastward. He had expected to see pursuing horsemen. They were not in sight. Surely the Crows must have missed the twenty horses. Their trail over the frosted plains would be easy to follow. Perhaps the Crows were afraid to come any farther westward, into the land of the Gros Ventres and Pecunnies now that these tribes were at peace. Nevertheless, the Crows were brave warriors. They had many guns, many more than the Gros Ventres or Pecunnies. They might yet follow him. He felt grateful for his lead. The Crows would have to ride fast to catch him now.

Not until midday did Wolf let the horses rest. Stopping

them in a meadowy grove beside the river, he left Breath-feather to herd the animals, climbing a knoll to watch the plains. The tough little horses, too weary to require herding, began at once to crop grass against another drive which they seemed to know was coming. Not until she saw Wolf coming leisurely from the knoll did Breath-feather unpack the remaining pemmican.

Dancing about her, Wolf boasted now, belittled the Crows, telling the story of the sleeping herder, getting down on his hands and knees to reenact his surprising discovery of the unconscious Crow, laughing happily at his own sudden fear. "Ahh!" he whispered, suddenly serious, his hands uplifted. "The Winds saved that Crow's life. The Winds are strong Helpers, ahh!"

Then, his serious mood vanishing as quickly as it had come, Wolf seized Breath-feather, dancing, singing, until she protested. "Not so loud, Wolf," she cautioned, glancing apprehensively over his shoulder.

"Ho, Woman!" he cried, pretending pique. "Twenty horses! Twenty good Crow horses for one pretty girl? No! I will send you back to your father and *keep* the horses. Shall I?" he asked, again seizing her playfully.

"No," she whispered, her arms about his neck. "No, Wolf. But do not give my father twenty horses. Give him fifteen. Let us keep five ourselves. We shall need them."

"Are you worth no more than fifteen Crow horses?" he teased her, as though the value of Crow horses had suddenly dropped.

"Maybe," she answered, coquettishly, giving him pemmican, her further witchery delaying their meal until Wolf saw that they must push on.

Out on the plains again, the horses rested, Wolf and Breath-feather traveled fast until they had reached country which was often used by their people. There was little to fear from the Crows now, and yet more than once Wolf climbed knolls to look backward.

Should he give Red-moccasin all the horses, the twenty head, or should he keep five, as Breath-feather had suggested? He well knew that in such cases custom demanded him to give Red-moccasin all horses and all property taken in his first raid upon an enemy after stealing his daughter. Could he break this custom? He had already broken custom. Yes, and perhaps he had broken the peace. Was he, in the eyes of his tribesmen, a traitor? Would they kill him? Would the whole village turn against him? Where was the village now?

Wolf knew that the Gros Ventres would be hunting buffalo on the plains, making their kill of winter meat. But the plains were wide, endless, and he had seen no buffalo. The great herds of buffalo must be farther west. The Gros Ventres would be near them. When he found the village, should he ride into it with his stolen horses, give them to Red-moccasin, who might reject them, leaving him in an even more embarrassing position? Or should he hide until he could somehow give the horses to the war chief by stealth, tying them to his lodge in the night? This last intrigued him, even though he knew that the feat would be difficult. Twenty horses, or even fifteen, were too many to handle alone in such an undertaking. He had never known of his people killing a fellow tribesman. Perhaps he had better ride straight into the village. But first he would camp, letting the horses rest so that they might make a good appearance. They were tired now.

Before sundown, thrilled and a little frightened by the sight, Breath-feather was first to discover the village. Far off in the light of the setting sun she saw the Gros Ventre lodges. She called to Wolf, who at once turned the horses toward the river, hoping that the ever-watching village sen-

tinels had not seen them. Heart and soul, Wolf was a Gros
Ventre. Now, despite possible differences between himself
and them, he felt his blood warming at their nearness.

Startled by the horses entering a meadow, a deer
bounded to the edge of surrounding bushes, stopping to
stare curiously at the intruders. An arrow from Wolf's bow
sent the creature leaping away, mortally wounded. "Ho,
Woman, we will feast," he exulted, rounding up the horses
in the meadow before following the deer. When he had
gone, taking a horse to pack the meat, Breath-feather made
their bed; and then she gathered small, dry cottonwood
limbs which make little smoke in burning. Not until after
sundown did Wolf return with the deer. And yet, fearing
that the Gros Ventre sentinels might see its smoke, they
did not kindle their fire until dusk, carefully selecting a
spot shielded by bushes beside the river.

Roasting the meat before their first fire, they feasted,
whispering happily, until they could eat no more, Wolf reciting humorous incidents of his raid upon the Crows,
chuckling merrily over the serious antics of the wolfskin so
near the sleeping herder. "It nearly blinded me. If The
Winds had not stopped me, I might have bumped the
Crow's moccasins with my nose," he laughed, slapping his
knee. "We have been lucky. The Winds have helped us," he
ended, his arm about the girl's waist.

When their fire had burned low, feeling joy in this,
her first real household duty, Breath-feather skinned the
rest of the deer, cutting up the meat for ready packing.
"Ho," she said, happily, "we shall not return to the village
empty-handed. Horses and meat! What more could any
man ask for?"

"A woman, of course, a pretty woman," Wolf said, kissing her. "Meat is everywhere," he told her. "Horses are

plentiful if a man is not lazy. But to get a pretty woman a man must——"

"*Steal* her," she interrupted, darting away from the nearly dead fire, knowing that Wolf would follow. Round and round the dark meadow they raced like carefree children, the tired horses stirring restlessly until, captured, the breathless girl offered Wolf her laughing lips.

Near morning the loose horses began moving toward the plains, their departure causing one of the staked animals to whinny, awakening Wolf. "Sleep on," he whispered to Breath-feather, getting up to turn the band back to the meadow. Fearing that if he slept again the horses might stray too far, Wolf wrapped his robe about him, watching the animals until dawn.

The stars told him that daylight was not far off. When the morning came, he must move, know exactly what to do. He had not once spoken to Breath-feather of his fear that their people might call him a traitor. In his mind he was anything but a traitor. He would gladly die for his people. Somehow he could not believe that they would condemn him for killing the man who had slain his brother. He had little fear of Breath-feather's father, even though he knew that Left-hand had poisoned his mind. If Red-moccasin refused to accept the horses in payment for his daughter, he, Wolf, would steal more, and more again, until, shamed, the war chief relented. He would, in the morning, ride into the village before the hunters started out to kill buffalo. He would leave Breath-feather here in the meadow until he had settled with her father, first offering him fifteen horses. If he refused them, the remaining five might win him over. If not, well, he would then visit the Crows again, even if he had to go to their country on the Yellowstone River.

Before the dawn Wolf aroused Breath-feather, telling her his plan. "Keep yourself and the horses hidden," he said. "I shall be back before the sun is in the middle of the sky. I shall be hungry, because today I will eat no meat with anybody but you." And then, fondly kissing the girl, Wolf set out for the Gros Ventre village, driving fifteen horses ahead of him.

Chapter 19

Upon gaining the plains, turning the horses westward, Wolf thrilled at the first touch of the morning breeze from the east. "Ho, my Helpers, I thank you," he fervently shouted to space, lashing the horses when he saw that the Gros Ventres had discovered him in the growing light. Singing loudly now, the timbre of determination, joy, and anxiety in his song, Wolf sent his rope's end popping at the horses again and again until, unchallenged, they clattered into the village, men waving their greeting, women peering curiously from lodge doors, many stepping outside to see, to talk excitedly to neighbors.

Glancing neither right nor left, Wolf dashed straight to Red-moccasin's, circling the stolen horses round the chief's lodge. "Ho, Father-in-law," he called loudly, "I am here to pay for my woman. Come out and care for these horses."

Men, walking rapidly, drew nearer. Women gathered in groups, talking, whispering, wondering, until the war chief stood beside Wolf's panting horse.

"Red-moccasin," Wolf said, his voice calm, his eyes looking into the chief's, "I promised that if you would give me your daughter I would tie ten good horses to your lodge before the green grass came again to the plains. You would not listen. Because I love her, I stole Breath-feather. Now, instead of ten horses, I offer you fifteen."

Ignoring the eyes of many watchers, Red-moccasin turned his head, quickly appraising the proffered gift. Horses were scarce with the Gros Ventres since the Pecunnies had raided. "Where is my daughter, Wolf?" he asked, his voice nearly friendly.

"My woman, the only woman I shall ever have, is waiting for me," Wolf answered. "Do you accept my gift? Shall I bring my woman?" he asked, as though he cared little what the answer might be.

"Yes, my Son, bring Breath-feather to our village. I accept the gift. Bring your woman," the chief answered.

Wolf saw happiness glow in the eyes of Breath-feather's mother, who was standing behind Red-moccasin. But custom forbade him speaking to her now. He would never again speak to her, nor she to him, since the woman had suddenly become his mother-in-law.

"Ho!" he said, leaning from his horse to shake Red-moccasin's hand, "I will bring my woman, Father-in-law. We will hunt for meat together, you and I," he said, as though they had never disagreed.

Dismounting, Wolf led his horse toward his mother's lodge, stopping many times to talk with friends. All were glad of his return, none mentioning the one-eyed Flathead, their heartiness and forbearance shaming Wolf for his distrust. Never again would he doubt the fairness, the loyalty of his people.

In the lodge where his parents had been anxiously waiting Horned-bull, chuckling knowingly, as though some special ordinance had given only men the power to fully comprehend such moments, warmly greeted his son, proudly offering his pipe. Small-voice, her eyes alight with love and deeper understanding, asked first for Breath-feather. "My new winter lodge of cowskins is finished," she said. "I will pitch it beside our own for you and Breath-feather. Did the pemmican last?" she asked solicitously.

Before Wolf could answer, old Black-tongue entered, his wrinkled face wreathed with smiles. "Ho, ho, hyee!" he greeted, sitting down beside Wolf to smoke the pipe, chuckling with glee. "This is a great day," he said, passing the pipe to Horned-bull, "a great day for us all. Did the Crows offer you fight?" he asked Wolf.

"No," smiled Wolf, "they were sleeping."

"Ho! Sleeping? A man who owns a good horse or a pretty woman is a fool to sleep until he knows that you, too, are sleeping, my Son. Where is your stolen woman? I would look at her," laughed the old medicine-man, as though he would appraise Breath-feather as he would a horse.

"I will go and bring her to the village," Wolf said, rising. "She will be anxious to learn if we are to live with our people. I have been away from her too long."

"Wait, my Son," called Black-tongue, who had followed Wolf outside, "I would talk to you."

"Where is Left-hand?" Wolf asked, walking with the old man, leading his horse.

"The half-breed has gone to trade at Ford Benton with his followers at his heels," answered Black-tongue. "When he returns with bright blankets and other silly things, he may have another medicine-dream."

"Have you spoken of his lying, exposed him?" Wolf asked.

"No, my Son. The wind is yet blowing. The half-breed is popular. Many of our people believe in his dreams and prophecies. He has said his medicine has told him that your killing the one-eyed Flathead will bring trouble to the Gros Ventres. You must watch Left-hand. He may mistake you for an enemy some dark night. This is the thing I wished to say to you."

"When I return to the village, when I shall have killed my winter's meat, I will ask you to tell me how you know that Left-hand lied about counting coup on the Pecunnie," Wolf said, ignoring the old man's warning.

"And when you ask, I will tell you, my Son," Black-tongue promised, as Wolf mounted his horse, wondering why Left-hand had hated him from the very beginning. What could have so quickly set the half-breed against him, a mere boy? However, he had never feared Left-hand, did not fear him now. His heart was too light, too happy, his gratitude to his people for their forgiveness too great to permit his mind to dwell upon Left-hand.

Waiting, anxiously watching the plains, Breath-feather was quick to see Wolf coming, coming back to her *without* the fifteen horses. Joy! Running to the meadow, the happy girl replenished her fire, carefully turned the roasting venison and then, placing a wreath of yellow leaves upon her head, dashed back to the plains to meet her man, her eyes shining with excitement and love. Singing of victory, his wild song punctuated by sharp, wolflike yelps, Wolf rode round and round the little meadow, the joyous girl dancing before him until suddenly leaping from his horse he seized her in his arms. "Ho, my Woman, my heart-woman," he said, kissing her lips, "your father accepted the horses. Now let us feast."

"And we have six horses ourselves," Breath-feather reminded him, leading him to the fire. "Eat, feast," she laughed. "You have earned a feast."

"Sit close to me, Breath-feather," Wolf said, making room by the fire. "You are now my woman, my only woman. I am your man, and we are both good horse thieves. Good horse thieves should always sit close together when they eat."

"But they will whisper, talk about you, Wolf, if you act like this when we are in the village," she said, sitting down beside him, her eyes shining.

"Let them whisper; let them talk. Eat, Woman. We must go to the village. I must kill our winter's meat while the buffalo are yet fat," he answered, helping himself to the roasted venison.

But even after they had packed the horse, made ready to leave the little meadow, they lingered there as though loath to share their happiness with others, as though having discovered a new world they would rather occupy it alone. Somehow, intrigue, ostracism, loneliness, and danger seemed now to have sanctified their union so that when at last they rode toward the village both were silent, both fearing that renewed contact with their people might tarnish their remembrances of their flight.

And yet, when they entered the village, those fears were allayed. Their lodge, new and white among its grimy neighbors, its fire burning cheerfully, the tender, heartfelt greeting of Small-voice, the forgiveness of Red-moccasin spoken in presenting his war shield to Wolf, the many callers, the feasting, and the presents so warming their hearts toward their people that they wondered at their earlier fears. Small-voice, last to leave the lodge, held Breath-feather in her arms a moment before bidding her good night. Remembering that the girl's mother was forbidden by custom to visit her daughter's lodge when her man was present, she said, "You must see your mother before you sleep, my Daughter."

"Yes. I had not forgotten," the girl answered, following Small-voice outside. "I am going to see my mother now," she said, walking rapidly to the lodge of Red-moccasin. But her visit there was not overlong. Just now, when she wished so much to be alone with her mother, the presence of her father's other wives so embarrassed her that she returned to her own lodge.

"Oh, Wolf, we are *so* happy, *so* rich, that I am afraid," she said, kneeling before him, her arms holding a new buckskin gown and several pairs of pretty moccasins which her mother had given her. "See, Wolf! Look," she whispered, excitedly spreading the many gifts upon a robe in the firelight, her eyes as bright as the fire.

"Yes, they are fine, and we *are* rich, richer because we are forgiven, because the hearts of our people are not against us. I love our people," Wolf said, his voice soft with gratitude.

"And you saved me, Wolf," Breath-feather whispered, her head upon his shoulder.

Putting his arms around her, Wolf kissed her passionately. "I will hunt buffalo tomorrow," he said, as though the commonplace had suddenly intruded. Sitting together, they gazed, without speaking, at their lodge fire until long after the village slept.

A wolf howled near the tall lodges, challenging the village dogs. "The night is old," Breath-feather whispered, spreading their robes.

"Yes," Wolf answered, his thoughts far off. "Someday," he whispered, "we shall again run away together."

Chapter 20

For days and days, in the marvelous sunlight of the late fall, the Gros Ventres hunted buffalo on the plains, racks of fresh meat reddening their village where busy women, continually scolding saucy magpies and slinking dogs, both errant meat thieves, dressed robes and gossiped near their lodges.

Wolf had quickly killed the meat he needed but continued hunting, helping men whose need for meat was great. Because Wolf would not trade with the white man, Breath-feather's work was comparatively light. They needed few robes, none for trading. Breath-feather had easily dried their winter's meat. Nevertheless, because she hoped to keep the overburdened women from chattering, she was busy as a bee, spending her spare time at beautifying her lodge, making linings for it and a backrest for Wolf while the hunters were on the plains. But the women did talk, whispering as Breath-feather knew they would. "Wolf sometimes brings wood and water to their lodge as though his woman had been crippled. But Wolf is odd, has always been different from the others. Remember how he loved his brother, how he used to sing to him? Ah, yes, but his brother was a man. Wolf will soon tire of Breath-feather.

He will take another woman before two snows have gone. You will see. Men are as nearly alike as mice. Yes."

Breath-feather, proud of Wolf, hating everything that might belittle him in the eyes of his fellows, felt this talking as keenly as though it had all been addressed to herself. Wolf ignored it, laughing when Breath-feather told him what the women were saying. "A man should choose his customs as he does his weapons. Let them talk," he said, with finality.

Twice, to be nearer the herds, the village had moved; and then, as they sometimes did, the buffalo suddenly disappeared from the northern range overnight. Nearly enough meat had already been taken, and yet, as is always the case where there are many hunters, some of the older men needed more. Black-tongue was one of these. To help the old man, Wolf went with him and others, going north to again find buffalo. Red-moccasin, Horned-bull, and two other men, believing that they would sooner locate a herd of buffalo by going eastward, down the river, traveled in that direction. They never returned to the village. Their dead bodies were found two days later in a grove of cottonwoods beside the river by Wolf and a small war party. The four men had been ambushed by the Crows, shot down while eating in the grove, the site of the surprise attack, the position of the bodies and other details which only an Indian would notice telling the meager story of the party's destruction. After a careful survey of the scene Wolf, burning for battle with the Crows, believing that they were yet on the plains north of the Missouri, led his men on down the river, heading for their own territory. To follow them now, so far behind, even though the Crows were laden with buffalo meat, might lead Wolf and his men into the enemy's country, where the odds against them would be too great. Sending two men back to the village with the sad tidings of the death of the war chief and his companions, Wolf, returning to the grove beside the river, made travois and then, leading the burdened horses, transported the dead men to the village, his own heart torn by grief.

This tragedy, directly affecting Breath-feather, his mother, and himself, had so suddenly descended upon him that even when he reached the village he was unprepared to meet the two wailing women. Their piteous mourning so wrung his heart that he knelt with them, a single robe covering their heads and his own, sobbing like a little child.

As though the tragedy of the cottonwood grove had brought death to its every lodge, the whole village mourned for Red-moccasin, its war chief. He had been a brave warrior, a wise leader. Even though he had been ambitious, most men believed that he had been fair. Like all other Indian chiefs of the northern plains, Red-moccasin's necessary generosity to his tribesmen had kept him impoverished, so that now there was little for his heirs; and, of course, nothing for his women, who would now belong to his oldest brother if he would accept them. However, the Gros Ventres were not considering Red-moccasin's property. Even in their grief they were thinking most of immediate vengeance against the Crows.

The dead having been buried, a strong war party began forming, asking Wolf to *carry the pipe,* to be its leader. But to the astonishment of the younger warriors, who had been most instrumental in the movement, Wolf restrained them. "Let us wait until we have pitched our winter village," he advised. "There are fifteen young men at Fort Benton with Left-hand," he said. "Some of these will wish to go with us. After we have made our winter camp, I will go with you; and if you wish, I will *carry the pipe.*"

"Good," said the older men, who until now had looked upon Wolf as a hothead, "we will wait." And now, because they knew that he was both brave and generous, Wolf's counsel, showing thought and discretion, led these older warriors to think of him as Red-moccasin's successor, so that when the Gros Ventres had pitched their winter village, many men, both old and young, were talking of Wolf as war chief.

There was no such thing as hereditary leadership among the Indians of the northern plains. A son, if he possessed the necessary requirements, might follow his father as chief in any tribe, and not otherwise. Furthermore, with these plains people who individually gave their allegiance only to the deserving, withdrawing it at their individual discretion, a chieftainship, even though not readily won, was easily lost. Red-moccasin had several sons. None was now mentioned as war chief. Wolf, who knew of the talking, not being ambitious, did nothing to strengthen his candidacy, even after he had listened to Black-tongue.

"I am young, too young," he said, when the old man urged him to show interest in the efforts of his friends. "I shall not seek this office. If the council chooses me, I will serve all who will follow, all who will forbear to trade with the White men, all who will heed the warning of my medicine-dream."

"Many have already heeded this warning. Some, even of those who would willingly follow you as war chief, will not listen, will yet trade with the white man," old Black-tongue told Wolf. "Left-hand has many followers," he reminded, adding, "The half-breed is growing stronger. Many men believe in his medicine. He is dangerous; but with you as our war chief, Left-hand would be more careful."

At his request the old medicine man told Wolf how he

had learned that Left-hand had lied about counting coup upon the Pecunnie. "The blood on the horse told me that the half-breed had lied," he said. "The Pecunnie was riding *away* from the White man's fort, not *toward* it, when Left-hand shot him. It was not his medicine that told Left-hand the Pecunnie was coming to the Teton crossing. The Pecunnie was in the White man's fort. The half-breed *saw* him there. Then after making fools of our people, he waited for the Pecunnie at the crossing. The rest I have guessed. The white trader must have known that the White Chief was coming to make peace. He must have told Left-hand this. The cunning half-breed pretended to dream, prophesying the peacemaking. When he returns from his trading at Fort Benton, Left-hand will have another dream, make another prophecy. If he does, if he dreams again so soon after visiting his friend, the White trader——Ahh, he is coming now!" Black-tongue pointed to the plains. "Another medicine-dream, wearing a new red blanket, is approaching. Come to my lodge and smoke with me, Wolf."

Upon entering the winter village which had been pitched beside the Missouri, where wood and shelter from winter winds were available, the boisterous party was shocked to instant silence by the news of the death of Red-moccasin and the others, the young men moving about among the people as though half-ashamed of their newly purchased blankets and guns. Nevertheless, Left-hand began to hint covertly that the tragedy had been visited upon the Gros Ventres because of Wolf's action at the treaty making. When he learned that sentiment was strong to make Wolf war chief, the half-breed grew bolder, openly warning the people against choosing any man for war chief who had not signed the peace. His declaration that Wolf's killing the one-eyed Flathead would bring the tribe serious trouble was not new, however. Left-hand had made this declaration on the night following the killing. He had said then that his medicine had told him to warn the Gros Ventres of this trouble. Remembering the half-breed's great prophecy, the people had been impressed, some of them frightened. Now the half-breed himself, frightened by Wolf's popularity, determined to again demonstrate the power of his *God-medicine.*

At sundown the next day a crier rode about the village summoning the council's members to meet at dark. Lefthand had dreamed. He would tell the council many strange things which he had learned in his dreaming. Men changed their clothing, dressed their hair, glancing often at the fading light of day while their wide-eyed women hurriedly prepared the evening meal. Life in winter villages was likely to be vapid, feasting and storytelling furnishing diversion, and yet here, now, in this new winter village life was already offering excitement. They would hear the halfbreed. He was a good talker. Always they found delight in listening to good talkers, even though they might not agree with them.

At dark the council lodge, brightened by a cheerful fire, was filled with warriors who rightfully had seats there, the pipe passing four times before Black-tongue, the master of ceremonies, bade Left-hand to speak. Rising, the halfbreed moved to a point directly in front of Black-tongue.

"I have dreamed," he began, avoiding the old medicine man's eyes. "My medicine has told me that a white man's boat is tied to the river bank at the Rocky Point. In my dream I saw this boat. Men pull it up the river by strong ropes. They hoped to pull this heavy boat to Fort Benton, but because the water is low, they cannot reach the fort. They have tied the boat at the Rocky Point. I saw it in my dream. It is loaded with blankets, axes, powder, lead, guns, and many things we need if we are going to fight the

Crows. My medicine has told me that nobody, no other man in the world, knows that this trader boat is tied up at the Rocky Point. My Helpers have promised me that if I lead you to this boat the white men will trade with us there, giving more for our robes then we can get by going to Fort Benton. In the morning I will lead all who will go to this boat at the Rocky Point. I have finished."

In the silence that followed, Black-tongue filled and lighted the pipe, offering it to the Sky and the Earth before passing it to his left as the Sun travels. Left-hand, who had no right to sit in the tribal council arose to leave the lodge. "Wait! Sit down again. I will speak when we have smoked," the old man said, passing the pipe.

Putting the empty pipe aside, the medicine man arose, speaking only of the warning of Wolf's dream without once hinting of his suspicions concerning the source of Left-hand's information. "Already some of you have defied this warning," he declared, looking around the circle of faces in the firelight, his old eyes stern. Waxing eloquent, "I believe that the boat is tied up to the bank at Rocky Point," he said, leaning over the fire to look at Left-hand's face. "I believe that Left-hand will lead you to this boat and that the White men will trade with you there. But I tell you that if you again defy the warning of Wolf's great medicine dream disaster will quickly follow your defiance, that trouble will follow you from the boat to your lodges. I have finished."

Wolf, quick to understand the real import of the half-breed's shallow play, saw clearly that here was open defiance, not only of his medicine dream but of himself as a leader. In their avidity to possess the White man's guns and bright goods, many of the young men would be likely to listen now that the trading boat was so near.

"Ho!" he cried, springing to his feet. "Ho, Left-hand, your tongue is forked like that of a snake. You lie!" he said, striding around the fire to stand before the half-breed, his pointing finger nearly touching the man's nose. "You lied when you said that you had counted coup upon the Pecunnie. You lied when you said you had dreamed that the white men were coming to make peace. You lied about your medicine. Your medicine, itself, is a lie. You lie *now, again,* when you say you dreamed that the boat was at the Rocky Point. The white trader at Fort Benton *told* you that the boat was at Rocky Point, just as he told you the other things which you pretended to dream. You are a *liar,* half-breed, a liar and a *coward.* You should wear woman's clothes. Ho! I have finished."

Wolf had spoken slowly, deliberately, as though each word had been a blow intended to goad the half-breed to battle, the whitened, twitching lips of the craven inspiring in him inexpressible loathing. "Ho!" he smiled, glancing at Black-tongue, when Left-hand, as though suddenly released from torture, quitted the lodge.

For moments nobody spoke. Wolf's denunciation of Left-hand had so shocked the warriors that even when Black-tongue passed the pipe men accepted it blindly. Nevertheless, they knew that Left-hand had weakened beneath Wolf's searing words, many of them believing that they had been cunningly tricked by the half-breed.

"He will lead men to the boat in the morning," said Black-tongue, again filling the pipe, "and when he returns he will bring bad luck with him."

Chapter 21

Left-hand, now more than ever afraid of Wolf and yet hoping somehow to set the people against him, did his utmost to raise a large trading party to go to the boat at Rocky Point. Nevertheless, the story of Wolf's denunciation, which had instantly spread throughout the village, had so weakened the half-breed's standing that he could enlist only the young men who had gone with him to trade at Fort Benton, and not even all of these would follow him now. However, after a hasty skirmish to borrow or buy buffalo robes for their trading, twelve young men followed the half-breed from the village soon after daylight, their going exciting much unfavorable comment. Black-tongue, fanatically honest in his convictions, perhaps possessing some occult reason for his fear that the young traders would bring misfortune from the boat, was quick to weigh the sudden surge of sentiment against trading with white men which, in itself, must strengthen Wolf. Mounting a horse, even before the trading party was out of sight, the old man rode about the village, stopping here and there to repeat his warning of the night before, his half-chanted message, weird in the early light, awakening the minds of men to confusion and fear.

Superstition, the slavish servant of dread, had always

circumscribed these plains people. Breath-feather, kindling her lodge fire from a live coal which had been buried in the ashes, let her infant blaze die, leaning tensely forward to catch the words of Black-tongue, her eyes filled with sudden fear. "Did you hear, Wolf?" she asked, forgetting the fire.

"Yes," Wolf answered, gravely, sitting up in his robe as his mother entered the lodge.

"They will not listen, Wolf," Small-voice said, her hand brushing her eyes as though wiping away a remembered scene. "The people will not listen. I know, I know. And now you——"

She did not finish. Her abrupt change of mood and mien was as though some occult hand had forcibly sealed her lips. "Ahh," she sighed in unwilling resignation, sitting down by the door.

Ever since the death of Horned-bull, Wolf and Breath-feather had urged Small-voice to live with them. But she would not listen. "I am near, so near that I can ever hear your laughing," she had told them, her eyes merry. Now, with the feeling of need in her heart, Breath-feather again besought her mother-in-law to let one lodge be the home of the three.

"Not now, my daughter," she answered, her hand on the girl's head. "Not now. The day will come. It is——"

Again she stopped abruptly, this time turning the conversation to Black-tongue; and even though these plains people seemed to have understood the unwisdom of fostering fear by anticipation, the three talked earnestly of the old medicine man's warning before they breakfasted.

After Small-voice had gone from their lodge, neither Wolf nor Breath-feather mentioned the woman's apparent desire to foretell events which she believed would touch them both. Both understood and, deeply respectful of

Those Who Live Without Fire, dared not question their right to protect the unknown.

Nevertheless, their superstition sharpened by the woman's interrupted sentences, both Wolf and Breath-feather felt the torment of dread. And this dread, strengthened by ages of strange, weird experiences beyond their understanding, had spread among the people so that when the day's sun had set men were whispering fearfully of Blacktongue's warning.

Since September there had been no storm, no clouds. Now there came a fall of snow, whitening the plains beneath leaden skies. But this light snowfall, scarcely covering the short grass, would not last. Bright days beneath blue skies would come again when this snow melted away. Nevertheless, the snowstorm warned the Gros Ventres of the coming winter, of ice, of deep drifts, and of fierce blizzards out of the frozen north. However, the light snow and the leaden skies nurtured by cold winds held on until after fourteen days Left-hand and his party returned to the village.

They were not hilarious, and they were not burdened with trade goods. Trade whiskey had this time met their favor. Now most of them were repentant, two of them desperately ill. Before morning the two men died, their passing setting the whole village afire with apprehension. Within four days every member of the trading party, except Left-hand, who had had the disease, died of smallpox. Now apprehension became stark terror.

Nearly twenty years before, in 1837, this loathsome disease, brought to the plains by white traders, had scourged the tribe to near extermination. And yet, superstitiously believing that only the young men who had defied the warning of Wolf's dream would suffer now, the Gros Ventres were not seized by panic until scores of others had sickened, perishing so rapidly that in many lodges only the dead attended the dying. Bewildered, terrified by the speed of the spreading pestilence, young men made mad by the fevered sick, their carrion odor, stabbed themselves to death so that their own handsome bodies might escape such hideous scarring. Men and women of all ages beat upon drums, chanted, sang, invoking aid from their medicine, some pledging a sun dance. But even Black-tongue, who constantly visited the sick, was powerless to stay the sweep of the scourge. "Stay out of your lodges," the old man advised. "Build a great fire in the center of the village; build several fires. Stay near them." Never on the northern plains did a more hopeless people gather round fires. Fearful of even the touch of a friend's hand, men shrank from their blood brothers.

None in the stricken tribe doubted that the smallpox had come from the white traders on the boat at Rocky Point, nor that Left-hand had brought it to the village. None doubted that the scourge had been visited upon the Gros Ventres in punishment of their wrongdoing. Left-hand, whose medicine was strong, had told them that Wolf's killing the Flathead would surely bring them deep trouble. Was *this* his promised trouble? Or was the scourge punishing them for trading with white men, for defying the warning of Wolf's dream? Black-tongue had warned them against going to the boat. Left-hand, openly defying the old man, had gone to the boat, and now the Gros Ventres were hideously dying. Only fear of possibly offending *Those Who Live Without Fire* stayed the hands of the Gros Ventres against the half-breed.

Realizing his danger, knowing that unless he could somehow fasten the blame for the scourge upon Wolf the Gros Ventres would slay him, Left-hand resorted to trickery.

When he was a small boy with his parents in the white man's fort far down the Big River, he had more than once seen his white father perform a baffling trick for the entertainment of his guest. Once Left-hand managed the trick himself. He would use it now, use it to save his life. He must have a buffalo horn. These horns were everywhere, thousands of them. And yet no ordinary horn would answer his purpose. He must have a nearly straight horn, one that would stand upon its base, its larger end, without falling. It must be the horn of a young buffalo bull, short, stubby, and nearly straight. Finding such a horn, he carried it to his lodge, carefully trimming its base with his knife until its edges were smooth and straight and when placed upon a level plain would touch it all the way round the horn. Next, with the point of a small knife he drilled a tiny hole in the horn, about halfway between its base and its tip. Then, stripping several stringlike threads of inner bark from a dry cottonwood stick of firewood, he braided three of them together until the braid was as long as the horn, fastening the ends so that the braided strands would hold together. Now, with a lump of kneaded clay he stuck one end of the braided bark fast to the horn's small end, *inside*, so that it hung down exactly to the horn's lower edges like a clapper of a bell. Last, with his fingers he smeared melted tallow up and down the braided bark so that the touch of a blaze would set it burning instantly. It must not fail. His life depended upon these threads of cottonwood bark. He needed a small dish, a tiny pan with a flat bottom. He thanked his pagan god that he had traded for such a pan, an iron pan that would hold water. Making sure that the horn would stand, he placed it upright upon the pan's bottom. It stood up without falling; and yet his elation was not as great as his fear, now that he

157

was prepared for the trick. If it failed, the Gros Ventres would kill him, kill him instantly; and he knew that they would kill him if he did not try the trick.

Carefully placing the prepared horn outside his lodge where he could easily find it in darkness, he carried the pan to the largest fire, using it to drink water from a paunch kettle there. Then, dropping the pan beside the kettle, he left it for others to use if they chose. Now his stage was set. He waited only for night, his mind busily rehearsing every step, every motion that might add mystery to his trick. He dared not fail.

The ground about the blazing fires, wetted by the melted snow, trampled by so many restless feet, was muddy. Men and women, wrapped in robes, their moccasins soaked with muddy water, dared not leave the fires. All day and all night, as though they believed the intense heat would destroy the evil spirit of pestilence, sobbing women heaped wood upon the flames, their loved ones dying alone in their lodges. In their helplessness the very daylight seemed to mock these women, the nights to torture them. Tonight, when black darkness fell upon the village, many men were gathered round the largest fire, their grim faces drawn by grief and fear. Again they were listening to Black-tongue, who, now stricken by smallpox, could scarcely stand. "Ho," he cried, his feverish finger pointing at the half-breed's lodge door. "It was *he* who brought us this trouble, this sickness. It was Left-hand, the half-breed, the liar, the coward! Let him not escape. Strike him down!"

Wolf, seeing men draw their knives, stepped back from the fire. But even as his moccasined feet felt the chill of moving, he saw the enraged men stop in their tracks, their naked knives in their hands. Left-hand, his head bowed over the black ebony box that held his God-medicine, was coming to the fire, the men, awed by the half-breed's weird chanting, stepping aside to let him pass.

As though he had heard nothing of Black-tongue's repeated charge, had seen nothing menacing, the desperate man, kneeling before the fire, opened the black box, placed it upon the muddy ground, mysteriously chanting over the glinting gilded, agonized figure of Christ on the Cross.

Instinctively men fell away from it, their eyes wide with new fear. Never before had they looked upon Left-hand's powerful medicine. Now, afraid, they sheathed their knives to stare at the chanting half-breed. Suddenly Left-hand, lifting and covering his precious box, stood up, muttering to the fire, holding his hands in its smoke, brushing its blaze with his fingers. "Ho!" he cried, as though awakening from a trance. "Ho, my medicine has spoken, has told me how to prove to you that Wolf, and not I, brought this sickness upon you," he said.

"Do not move! Stand as you are until I find a buffalo's horn!" he commanded, running out of the firelight to return in a moment with his horn. Holding it first in one hand and then in the other above the blaze of the fire, alternately chanting and muttering incoherently, he was careful not to let the blaze touch the braided bark.

"Listen," he called, picking up the tiny iron pan. "You who have been lying, you who believe that I brought this sickness to our village, listen! I will pour water into this pan from this kettle. Then I will place this buffalo horn in the water in the pan. If the water goes into the horn when it is standing straight up, *Wolf, and not I,* brought this bad sickness upon our people. Ho!"

Stooping to pour the water, he deftly gathered enough thick mud to stop the hole which he had drilled in the horn, pouring a half pint of water into the pan. "Ho!" he called, swiftly passing the horn through the blaze of the fire, lighting the hidden bark. "Ho!" he exulted, his voice drowning a scarcely audible sound of gurgling. "Ho! Behold! The water has gone! It has entered the buffalo horn! *Wolf brought us this trouble!*"

Men pressed their hands upon their mouths in astonishment. Wolf, suspecting trickery, stepped nearer, his bright eyes flashing. But the half-breed, now sure of himself, dared to ignore him. "Come nearer, you who have been lying," he challenged. "Feel the bottom of this pan. Make certain that the water has gone into the horn."

When several men had gingerly brushed the pan's bottom, muttering as they looked at their dry fingertips, Lefthand dared to laugh. "Ho, you who have been lying, I will now show you that the water went into the horn when it was standing up straight, that the water is *yet* in the horn," he declared, his voice highly pitched.

Holding the horn tightly against the pan's bottom, Lefthand turned the whole upside down, lifting the pan from the horn. "See?" he sneered, thrusting the half-filled horn beneath the noses of the nearer men. "See, the water is in the horn! It will *wet* you, you liars!" he shouted, insolently dashing the water against their frightened faces, laughing fiendishly when the startled warriors fell back, wiping their eyes with their hands.

Contemptuously pitching the buffalo horn into the fire so that nobody might examine it, Left-hand walked to the now lifeless body of Black-tongue. "Here lies the man whose medicine could not save him," he sneered, pointing at the wretched form. "He lied, and you listened. You believed that his medicine was powerful, and yet he is gone, and I am still here. Ho!"

160

This was enough, more than enough. Wolf felt the accusing eyes of his people burning into his heart. Nevertheless, even as men pointed their fingers at him, his eyes were fixed upon Left-hand. Baffled, and yet certain that the cunning half-breed had again cruelly tricked his people, he darted to the fire. "Liar! Coward! Dog-face!" he cried, drawing his knife as the craven stepped backward. "Has your lying medicine made your heart strong enough to fight?" he asked, following the half-breed, his voice suddenly low and steady. "Fight, coward!" he challenged, slapping Left-hand's face, "or must I kill you as I would kill a defenseless rabbit," he whispered, his eyes blazing.

Wolf's attack had been so sudden that he had reached the half-breed before the men realized his intention. Now, afraid that Left-hand's death might offend *Those Who Live Without Fire*, they seized Wolf, who struggled vainly to reach the half-breed. "Let me go!" he cried, his shoulders frantically pushing his captors. "If he has not lied, if his medicine is not a lie, he will kill me. Let me go," he begged, the growing sneer on Left-hand's lips maddening him.

With a quick, twisting wrench Wolf freed himself for an instant, striking wildly with his knife at Left-hand, who, avoiding the blow, fell backward over a log of firewood. Seized again, his arms held tightly to his panting sides, Wolf's struggling suddenly ceased, his muscles relaxing. "Yes," he whispered, as a newborn Night Wind, heavy with putrid odors, swept toward him from among the stricken lodge. "I have finished," he said, simply, to his captors, his body dripping with perspiration.

Freed, Wolf swept the faces of his tribesmen with appraising glances. Both accusation and distrust lingered in their eyes. "I will go," he said, reading their thoughts; and then, hurt beyond expression by those for whom he would have given his life, he strode toward his lodge followed by the half-hostile eyes of several hundred men.

But his lodge was down, packed. Eight horses, five of them with heavily laden travois, were waiting in the night shadows where the lodge had stood. Rushing to meet Wolf, handing him his bow and quiver, Breath-feather threw her arms about his neck. "She, your mother, knew that this was coming," she sobbed on his shoulder. "Oh, Wolf, I saw. I heard! I was afraid, afraid that they would kill you. But she, your mother, was not afraid. She said that you would come."

"Yes," he whispered, kissing her, "and I have come my heart-woman." Then, pretending lightness, "And now we shall again run away together," he smiled.

"Yes, Wolf, I know. Lead on. I will follow," she said, mounting her horse.

BOOK TWO

Chapter 22

Accepting banishment, his heart heavy with pity for his suffering people, Wolf headed out onto the whitened plains, the two silent women and a single village dog following the travois beneath a blackened sky. Indifferent as to course, trusting his Helpers, the Winds, to direct him, he rode through the night as one asleep, his dazed thoughts upon Left-hand's trickery and his people's fear of the half-breed's medicine. Not once had he even turned in his saddle to look backward toward the stricken village, scarcely noting that he had been traveling northwest until his horse had stopped beside a familiar water hole at dawn. Here, as though suddenly aroused, he got down from his saddle, whispering his thanks to his Helpers, The Winds.

"Pitch the lodge," he signed to the women, making the motion of thrusting a lance into the snowy plains, the morning breeze bringing to his nostrils the odor of nearby buffalo. And yet this gratefully recognized promise of plenty could not lift the load from Wolf's heart. His hurt was too deep, too new, too nearly like the blow of Rain's death, which had all but broken his spirit. His only hatred was for Left-hand, the half-white man who had tricked his people. Strangely enough, this hatred seemed to Wolf to be a thing apart, a personal matter that was ages old. It could wait. He would contrive to meet Left-hand again. But even though he believed that *Those Who Live Without Fire* were punishing them for disregarding the warning of his medicine dream, the suffering of his people tortured him, thoughts of their staring, frightened eyes about the blazing fires in the village wringing his heart. He could not bring himself to speak. Even in attending the horses against their return to the village herd, he walked softly, as though an unnatural sound might be sacrilege. In the lodge the two women, suffering with him, spoke sparingly in the sign language, not once breaking the silence of the camp until on the morning of the fourth day Wolf chanted his medicine song. "Ho," he said, ending the song, his weary eyes brightening, "we will move toward the Pecunnies."

The sun, in a turquoise sky, had come again, melting the snow, so that by the time they had reached the mouth of the Marias on the Missouri River the plains were bare once more, the weather remaining clear and comfortable while they made their winter camp not far from the fire-charred ruin of the American Fur Company's Fort Piegan. Twenty-three years had passed since the Pecunnies had burned Fort Piegan, and yet this act of hostility had not driven the white traders from the country. Instead, they had only moved a little farther up the great river, building Fort Mackenzie where the traders, in cold blood, had murdered a band of visiting Pecunnies. Wolf, eight years old at the time, well remembered this hideous butchery and the subsequent burning of Fort Mackenzie by the incensed Pecunnies. But even this second exhibition of hostility had not stopped the white men. Again they had moved a short distance up the Missouri, finally building Fort Benton.

Now the Pecunnies and even Wolf's own people, the Gros Ventres, traded at the new fort as though nothing had happened, as though *Those Who Live Without Fire* had not warned them, through his medicine dream, to have nothing to do with white men. Even in his banishment, feeling that he had failed as the chosen envoy of *The Supernatural Ones*, Wolf found a little satisfaction in the ruins of these two forts of the powerful white men; and yet he entertained no thoughts of finding adherents to the warning of his great dream among any of the Blackfeet tribes. He had entered the domain of the Pecunnies for protection from both the Sioux and the Crows, whose war parties often raided the northern grasslands, even in winter. These two powerful tribes, constantly at war with each other, were mutual enemies of the Pecunnies and the Gros Ventres, who, after several years of strife among themselves, were again united against them. There had never been peace on the northwestern plains, and now Wolf, wandering alone about the ruined stockades of the two forts, recalled his own hasty action at the treaty ground and the lately healed feud between his people and the Pecunnies, thinking grimly of the frailties of peace agreements. To him the ruined forts were symbols of the White man's power and persistence, bringing to him the realization that without peace among the plains tribes, a strongly united front, the white man could not be stopped. And yet Wolf could not imagine such a peace. The very past forbade it. *Those Who Live Without Fire* had bidden him to warn his own people against dealing with White men. They had not mentioned the other tribes. But his people had not listened. Now, in his banishment, hoping that his own strict observance of his dream's warning might temper the wrath of his Helpers against his people, Wolf solemnly promised the Winds to live as his forefathers had lived, to avoid White men until he should go to the *Sand Hills*[1] forever.

The winter, a mild one with many chinook winds, was half gone before a band of Pecunnies discovered Wolf's lodge, their quick permission to remain in their territory giving him deep satisfaction. They had heard of the terrible plight of the Gros Ventres, expressing sorrow for the tribe. They knew Wolf's story, commending him for his constancy to his Helpers, and yet no Pecunnie offered to enlist in his cause. Wolf had not expected more, and yet, when the friendly Pecunnies rode away from his camp, his heart was heavy with the same feeling of loneliness that had come to him upon leaving Black-tongue's lodge after relating his medicine dream. But thoughts of the old medicine man brightened him. "Ho, Black-tongue, old warrior, good friend," he said beneath his breath, his eyes toward the *Sand Hills,* directly north, "I will live as *They* have bidden me. I will paint my lodge with the story of my medicine dream so that *They,* and *You,* and all who are wise may know that I have not forgotten. Ho!"

Spring came early to the plains that year, the water of the Missouri rising before the wild geese had begun their flight from the South to nest on the tops of dead cottonwood snags in the groves along the stream. Even the stoical buffalo, responding to the touch of the changing seasons, shed earlier than usual, rolls of their soft winter coats bobbing and bouncing over the greening plains to be caught and held by sagebrush or rosebushes. Reveling in the miracle of unfolding life, Wolf saw renewed assurance of the rightness of his course in the color change of every grassy knoll, every early blossom, and returned bird, only pity for his people precluding his complete happiness.

[1] The Heaven of the four federated tribes.—F. B. L.

Each day now Small-voice listened for the first call of the curlew, both Wolf and Breath-feather rejoicing in the woman's eagerness. But Wolf was first to hear the curlews. Awakened at dawn by the patter of rain upon the lodge skin, he caught the first glad piping of the returned birds. "Your friends have come, Mother," he said, sitting up in his robe. "The curlews are here."

"Ah!" Small-voice sat up, listening in the gray light. "Yes, yes, they have come. My friends are here again," she said happily. "I would go out on the plains to greet them if rain were not falling."

"This rain will not last, Mother," Wolf assured her. "There will be sunshine by the time we have eaten our meal, and then Breath-feather and I will go out on the plains with you, help you to welcome your friends."

Out on the plains beneath a sky of scudding clouds that cast patches of moving shadow upon the grass and clustered flowers, the three rode among flocks of curlews, Small-voice so perfectly imitating their notes that hundreds of the birds circled above her head, swooping, darting, piping about the happy woman as though glad of her welcome. Laughing as children laugh, the three rode on and on, countless curlews rising at their approach, Small-voice merrily calling birds from every flock until suddenly, out of a coulee just ahead, a score of wolves raced over a knoll top, some of them stopping at the crest to look back, their heads and ears sharp silhouettes against the sky.

"Ho!" cried Wolf, heading for the coulee with the women. "The wolves have been feasting. Let us see what they have killed."

Scattered up and down the long coulee Wolf counted seventy buffalo that had been killed for their tongues, not a robe having been taken. He could see that a small herd had been surrounded in the coulee by white men from

167

Fort Benton, clearly understanding how, in their bewildered milling in the coulee, the buffalo had been shot down for their tongues by the white men, who knew that robes were not prime now. Wolf had witnessed wasteful killing of buffalo by his own people. He had heard his father tell of their driving small herds over cliffs for winter meat and how the practice had been stopped by a Pecunnie's dream, which had warned the four federated tribes against such wanton slaughter. Often even now a man in need would kill a buffalo for a meal or two, and yet this slaughter by white men of seventy full-grown buffalo for their tongues alone made Wolf think seriously of the warning of his dream.

Thoughtfully he led the way back to the river, short showers of light rain brightening the wild flowers that were taller and more plentiful as he neared the swelling stream. Riding in single file behind him, Breath-feather and Small-voice were singing when they reached a grove of tall cottonwoods beside the Missouri, an hour's ride above their camp, the perfume of the opening leaf buds on the huge trees sweet in the moist air. Here the leaves of rosebushes, sparkling with raindrops, were half-grown, their tender green heightened by the gray trunks of the cottonwoods and red of willows. The grove, in a bend of the river, was not deep, so that, swinging downstream to ride along the grove's edge toward their lodge, the three caught occasional glimpses of the rising water beyond the trees, the women singing until Wolf, turning in his saddle, silenced them by holding up his hand.

Up the river a little way wild geese were honking excitedly, as though they had been flushed from the water, several pairs of the great birds circling high above the heads of the three riders, to speed away up the stream again. Something had frightened them, and when several flocks of mallards had followed the geese, Wolf dismounted, signing to the women, who, afoot, followed him into the grove. Concealing their horses among the red willows, the three found cover for themselves on the river's cutbank, all of them looking upstream, all of them thinking of their lodge, which was in sight from the river, and all expecting to see a canoe or boat bearing white men from Fort Benton. But even Wolf was not prepared to see the fleet of five mackinaws, each of them fifty feet long, that swept round the bend one by one, the current of the Missouri carrying the newly built boats toward far-off St. Louis as rapidly as a horse could trot.

Setting in against the cutbank where the three were hidden, the current swept the five mackinaws, one by one, directly toward them, the unpainted craft looming so large that the frightened women drew themselves backward, deeper into the screening willows. So near was each boat in passing that Wolf might have touched it with his bow, each astonishing him with its highly piled packs of buffalo robes and freight of dried tongues. "More than enough to last my people and all the Blackfeet from snow to snow," he thought bitterly when the five mackinaws passed from his sight down the river carrying twenty-one-thousand buffalo robes and buffalo tongues. Wolf well knew that most of these robes and many of the tongues had been traded in at Fort Benton by the Pecunnies and his own people, new realization of his inability to bring even the Gros Ventres to understand the danger of trading with white men so depressing him that he lay silent, his eyes upon the rising water of the river, the two patient women in the deeper bushes behind him not moving a finger until, closely skirting the river's bank, a flock of swift-flying teals aroused him.

"Ho!" he laughed merrily, rising to his feet, now determined that his lodge should be a place of happiness and plenty, that as long as he lived he would bear his own burden, sharing none of his fears with either Breath-feather or his mother. "Sing, sing!" he called, leading the way to their horses. "I shall paint my lodge with the story of my dream, and you, my mother, shall make the paint," he said, mounting.

Chapter 23

During the following June, the moon of roses, the Sun Dance moon, Wolf's lodge, now handsomely painted with the story of his medicine dream, was pitched in a land of teeming buffalo, a land of plenty skirting the beautiful Sweet Grass Hills. He had heard nothing of his people during the winter, and now north of the Marias, north of the Missouri, and far north from the Gros Ventres he saw only an occasional party of Pecunnies out searching for possible Crow encroachers, none of these possessing the news which he so much desired. To keep sorrow from his lodge, he seldom spoke of the Gros Ventres to the two women; and they, understanding, had followed his example in this so that in all of them there was a suppressed desire not only to learn of the fate of their people but to speak of them to others. And yet, when finally the opportunity came, none of them could ever forget its coming.

Wolf was out on the plains hunting buffalo when a Pecunnie warrior and his woman, on their way to visit a village of Bloods farther north, stopped at the painted lodge in the Sweet Grass Hills and told Small-voice and Breath-feather that the scourge of smallpox had taken nearly all the Gros Ventres.

"There are but seventy-five warriors left alive," the man declared, covering his face with his hands.

"And of our friends, the Gros Ventres, there are left seven women to one man, besides the children, besides the children of the dead," the Pecunnie woman sobbed, tears upon her cheeks.

Throwing her arms about Breath-feather, Wolf's mother sank to her knees. "Ah, the white man, the white man! His sickness is killing us. Wolf! Wolf, my son! Come to us, come to us," she wailed, her body trembling in the agony of grief.

Kneeling beside them, the Pecunnie woman, herself shaken by the news which she and her man had brought, tried to comfort the woman, her man moving away from the lodge and seating himself upon the grass with his back to the group.

Wolf, returning, instantly knew the reason for the wailing of Breath-feather and his mother, dreading to hear the story which he knew had been told by the visitors. Hastily dismounting from his horse, he spoke softly to the women before formally welcoming the Pecunnie warrior to his camp. Then drawing the man farther away from the lodge so that the women might not hear the story repeated, he questioned him, hoping to learn the names of the living Gros Ventre warriors. But the Pecunnie could name but few, Left-hand, the half-breed being among these.

"The Crows have twice attacked the few Gros Ventres who are left," the Pecunnie told Wolf, who at once determined to move southward so that he might be nearer his harassed people. Hope of soon meeting his cousin, Left-hand, was again uppermost in mind.

Guarding himself against an open expression of grief which would intensify the suffering of Breath-feather and his mother, Wolf waited four days after the Pecunnies had gone before moving south, his hope of again facing Left-hand growing into a firm resolution as he led the way toward the Marias. He had no intention of directly visiting the Gros Ventre village without a formal invitation, and yet he was determined to help his weakened people by acting as their scout against the Crows and Sioux, to warn them of approaching war parties, and to help them fight their enemies. Striking the Marias, he would follow the stream to its mouth and then go as far down the Missouri itself as he dared; and somehow he would contrive to meet Left-hand.

Reaching the mouth of the Judith, the two women pitched Wolf's painted lodge on the exact spot which had been occupied by his father's during the treaty making. But the treaty ground, the charred sticks of its dead fire, the jutting point on the river where Breath-feather had met Wolf, and the empty surrounding plains where the villages had stood so vividly reminded them of the fate of the Gros Ventres that they moved farther down the Missouri when daylight came. When they had reached a large cottonwood grove, not three days' journey from the mouth of the Musselshell, they pitched their lodge, the worried women herding the horses close to the camp since this was dangerous territory. Wolf knew that the present Gros Ventre village was directly north of him now, intending to remain in the vicinity throughout the summer unless forced to flee. Buffalo were so plentiful here that he could easily keep his camp supplied with meat, leaving him plenty of time to scout on the plains mostly across the river, where high knolls offered splendid stands from which to watch the surrounding country on both sides of the stream. But, excepting Gros Ventre buffalo runners far away on the north side of the river, he saw no human beings, the weeks dragging into the heat of late summer while he watched the plains for approaching Crows or Sioux, the monotony of constantly herding their horses near the cottonwood grove gradually overcoming the women's fear of attack.

September came, its gentle warnings of summer's passing reminding the women that their winter's meat must soon be prepared, and a suitable place selected for their winter camp, an early storm giving them an excuse to urge Wolf to start back up the river to safety. There had been rain, the weather cooling considerably, the grassy plains smelling fresh when Wolf took his station upon one of the high knolls across the river, having promised Breathfeather and his mother that he would lead the way up the stream on the following day. Near midday he saw two wolves trotting westward up the river on the north side, idly watching them as he had watched hundreds of others from the knolls. Suddenly the wolves stopped, their noses upon the moist ground as though smelling the tracks of some animal, both turning to follow the tracks toward the river a little way before leaving them to trot westward again. There was nothing extraordinary in this, but when a single wolf, going the other way, down the river and not far from it, stopped to smell the plains so near the water, Wolf was immediately interested. Something had traveled across the plains from the north. If there had been blood on its trail, the wolves would have followed it, even across the Missouri if it had crossed; and Wolf felt certain that it had.

First scrutinizing the plains in all directions to assure himself that no enemy was in sight, Wolf led his horse out of a coulee, riding down the river without crossing it. The trail which had interested the wolves had been made by horses. Wolf found their tracks in the mud where they had landed after crossing the stream. Getting down from his horse, he carefully examined them, trying to determine the number of horses that had climbed the muddy bank, knowing that they had been stolen from the Gros Ventres by Crows since the trail, after leaving the river, headed straight for the Crow country. He knew that the stolen horses had not long ago crossed the river because the water impounded within the tracks nearest the stream was yet roily. Following the shore downstream a little way, he found the tracks of two horses which he felt certain had been ridden by the thieves, who had crossed the river below the stolen horses, thus preventing any from turning back. This discovery delighted him, even though he knew that other riders might have crossed the river directly behind the stolen horses, which he believed numbered nearly twenty. Returning to the tracks of the stolen animals, he squatted beside them, stirring the roiled water in them with his finger, even fashioning a horse's track in the mud, watching it fill with muddy water, patiently waiting half an hour for it to clarify sufficiently to let him know more nearly the time of the crossing. "Since daylight," he whispered, happily knowing that during the day at least the thieves would conceal the stolen horses, hiding themselves until night. He believed that the horses had been stolen by two Crows, probably young warriors out to gain their first distinction, and that they were not far away.

Blaming himself for having been much later than usual in reaching his stand this morning, Wolf took up the trail, following it rapidly until he saw ahead of him a succession of high knolls and deep coulees. The sun was yet high when, as he rode to the top of a small knoll, an object on the summit of a higher knoll ahead caused him to stop, turning his horse back. Guessing that the suspicious object would prove to be a Crow sentinel and fearing that the man might have seen him during the moment he had been in sight, Wolf dared not look again from the knoll. Instead, he dismounted, leading his horse back down the hill, carefully crossing the coulee at its base to another knoll which was nearer the object. Tying his horse's head down to the animal's fetlock with his bridle rope, Wolf crept to the knoll's summit, covering his head with his wolfskin before daring to look toward the other knoll. One glance sufficed. A Crow, facing north toward Wolf, sat upon the knoll top, no other man, no horses in sight. All this was natural. The other Crow, or perhaps a half-dozen other Crows, and the stolen horses would be in the coulee beyond the knoll; and the other Crow, or the half-dozen other Crows, would be sleeping, or they should be sleeping. If the Crows were not already so near their own territory, Wolf would have waited, watching them set out at nightfall so that he might be certain if there were two or more Crows. But he dared not wait. Another's day ride would bring the Crows to their own country. Wolf hastily planned to creep around the base of the Crows' knoll, depending upon his belief that there were but two of the thieves and that the one on the far side would be sleeping. Once on the far side, he would creep carefully up the knoll and kill the sentinel, taking his chance with the other in the coulee below.

"Where are you, Winds?" he whispered anxiously, setting out as soon as he felt the first breath of air on his naked back. Managing to get among the horses unnoticed, he began to creep up the knoll, his bow strung tightly, ready for instant use. He was near the top and directly below the Crow sentinel when a colt among the stolen horses plunged wildly through the band, whinnying loudly.

Instantly the sentinel dashed down the knoll, nearly running against Wolf who sent a ready arrow into his breast, the stricken crying out as he fell.

Quickly turning to face the coulee, another arrow notched to his bowstring, Wolf saw a young Crow warrior leap upon a horse, racing away without even glancing behind him.

The battle was finished. There was no need for hurry now. Thanking his helpers, The Winds, for his success, Wolf secured his own horse, starting the stolen animals back toward the Missouri, urging them to a lively trot.

The sun had set when he drove the horses across the river, wondering why the laggard Gros Ventres had not followed the Crows. Deciding to drive the horses to his lodge, holding them there until daylight, he had turned them up the river when he saw horsemen coming toward him from the north, Gros Ventres, ten of them, riding fast. They had seen Wolf and the horses. Believing that they had overtaken the thieves, they deployed, yelling madly, one of them firing a shot at Wolf, which was high, the ball whistling above his head. Raising his bow, he called to them, making the tribal sign.

The meeting, surprising to the embarrassed Gros Ventres, was satisfying to Wolf, who, after greeting his people, did not mention the shot. "You are slow. Have you been sleeping?" he said good-naturedly, scanning the faces about him, hoping to see his cousin there.

They were young men, all of them, none offering to smoke with Wolf, who, even though he burned to learn the names of the older Gros Ventres who were yet living, asked few questions. By right the stolen horses now belonged to him, and yet he said: "I give you these horses, and I also give you this Crow scalp. Dance with it. Who is your war chief?" he asked, guessing the answer.

"Left-hand. He, with three others, have gone to Fort Benton to trade for powder and ball," a young man replied.

"Ho!" said Wolf, mounting his horse to ride to his lodge up the river, thinking happily that Fort Benton was also up the river. He would travel rapidly and far in that direction. Perhaps he might meet Left-hand on the way. He would try.

Chapter 24

The failure of the young Gros Ventres to offer the pipe to Wolf after his service of recovering the horses from the Crows hurt him deeply. Here was evidence that his people had not relented, that Left-hand's power over them had not abated. Nevertheless, perfectly understanding his people's reason for their attitude toward him, Wolf did not blame them. He would continue to help them, believing that by removing Left-hand he would be serving them most. He would move in the morning before daylight, move up the river, finally pitching his lodge on the stream's farthest-north bank. Here he would be in the direct line of travel between Fort Benton and the Gros Ventre village. Here he could wait for Left-hand. He could reach the desired point on the Missouri's northernmost bend by traveling three long days, perhaps having to make one dry camp on the way since he would cut straight across the plains.

The stars were bright, a chill wind blowing when Wolf reached his lodge, his arrival relieving the women, who had anxiously looked for him since sunset. Sketchily telling the story of his day's adventure, without once mentioning Left-hand or the coolness of the young Gros Ventres toward him, he delighted Breath-feather and his mother by his evident anxiety to move westward before daylight.

Leaving the camp in the cottonwood grove where the Missouri turned suddenly south for a short distance, Wolf headed straight across the plains for the stream's northernmost point, camping at sundown of the second day on Eagle Creek, not far above the spot where Rain, his brother, had met death at the hands of the one-eyed Flathead. Never before had the women traveled so rapidly with travois, Small-voice protesting against Wolf's riding so far in advance. But Wolf, more eager than ever to intercept Left-hand, insisted upon speed. There was no need of any Gros Ventre traveling at night so near the Pecunnies, and if left-hand and his companions traveled in daylight, Wolf felt certain that the half-breed could not escape him now.

"Ho, sleepy ones!" he called teasingly before dawn of the third day. "This will be our last drive. Waken! Waken, lazy ones," he laughed, rolling Breath-feather from her robe. "I will bring in the horses," he told her, going out of the lodge.

"There is some hidden reason for all this haste, daughter," Small-voice said, beginning to take down the lodge while Breath-feather prepared the morning meal.

"Yes, Mother," the young woman agreed, feeling glad that they were traveling westward. "Wolf has seen something, or heard something that has made him hurry."

"It is something that he has heard, and he heard it from our people, the Gros Ventres," Wolf's mother said, folding the lodge skin. "And yet we are traveling westward, away from our people," she muttered, tying the bundle.

Near sundown their destination was in sight, the dark grove of cottonwoods gladdening the women. Wolf, riding far in advance of the travois, his eyes eagerly searching the plains, saw three horsemen round the timbered point on the river ahead. Turning in his saddle, he signed to the women. "Travel straight to the trees," he told them, drawing two arrows from his quiver before riding swiftly to intercept the horsemen.

"Ha! Now we know why we have been traveling like frightened antelope," said Small-voice, shading her eyes to stare at the three horsemen and her speeding son.

"Yes, yes. And Wolf drew arrows from his quiver, Mother. I saw him. I saw him draw them," Breath-feather said, her frightened eyes upon her man. "And they are Gros Ventres. They are our people," she added, her voice unsteady.

The horses had stopped, were cropping the grass. Suddenly, as though a mysterious message had reached them, the women faced each other, and there was understanding in the eyes of both.

"Left-hand!" Breath-feather faltered.

"Yes, Left-hand, the lying half-breed," husked Wolf's mother, drawing the young woman to her. "Have no fear, daughter. Wolf will kill him," she whispered, with deep conviction.

Wolf had reached the horsemen now. The four were huddled. Wonderingly the worried women saw the four, evidently friendly, ride eastward together. Finally stopping, they got down from their horses.

"They are smoking," Small-voice said, as though relieved of a heavy burden.

"Yes," agreed the younger woman, "all is well. Wolf is smoking with our people. Let us go on as he told us."

There was fire in the lodge when Wolf reached it, fire and boiled buffalo meat. "Ho!" he said, sitting down at the head of the lodge. "Left-hand is dead, killed by a white man at Fort Benton."

"Good!" Small-voice danced about the lodge. "The White killer did you a service, my Son," she laughed, stooping to hand Wolf a buffalo tongue from the kettle.

"Yes, it is good, Mother. Today I would have killed Left-hand even if he had been with fifty friends," Wolf smiled. "And instead, today I smoked with my people. Their hearts are not against us now that Left-hand is gone," he told them, happily.

"Sing, Wolf, sing." Breath-feather handed Wolf his drum, and he sang the owl song, the two dancing women joining in the singing.

Now they all had hope of again living with their people. But the winter passed without a word from the Gros Ventres reaching them. Twice during the winter parties of Pecunnies visited them; and once, near spring, they visited the Pecunnie village farther west, feasting on these happy occasions, both Small-voice and Breath-feather enjoying the contacts with other women.

Early in the summer, wishing to be nearer his people, Wolf again moved down the river, but not so far this time. Never more than a day's ride from the Gros Ventre village, he, and even the women, frequently saw Gros Ventre hunters now, sometimes talking with them. All were friendly enough, and yet none offered to enter Wolf's painted lodge, nor did any propose that Wolf move his lodge to the village. Nevertheless, from this time onward for years, never insinuatingly near, moving only when the Gros Ventres moved, Wolf's painted lodge, like a protecting jinn, was never far from the village, always pitched between it and its enemies, its very presence inspiring their respect, if not fear, of its master, whose story was known by all the surrounding tribes. It had become a plains tradition.

And yet the Gros Ventres did not relent. Under Left-hand they had learned to trade freely with white men. There was yet no sign that Wolf's dream was truly prophetic, no perceptible change on the grasslands. Wolf's dream could not have been a warning to the tribe. The red men, who were many, had never depleted the plains, had not even made the least impression upon them. Then how could the white men, who were few, devastate the grass-lands, wipe out the buffalo that had always increased in number each year since the world began? Thus the Gros Ventres argued among themselves; and, having been in-spired by Left-hand, they still believed that Wolf's killing the Flathead during the treaty making had brought the scourge of smallpox to the tribe.

Pretending indifference toward all this, free as an eagle, with an abundance of food and material for clothing and shelter upon every hand, never visiting Fort Benton, never trading with white men, Wolf often devoutly thanked his Helpers, the Winds, for their blessings, more than once beseeching them to send him children, brightening Breath-feather's heart. And yet no children came. Like himself, Breath-feather was growing older. Wolf had lately noticed this, and now he counted the snows which had passed since they ran away together, ten of them. "Ten snows," he murmured, remembering that his mother's hair was turning gray. Breath-feather's mother had been taken by the scourge, but Wolf's mother had taken her place. If there were children in their lodge, they, all of them, would be perfectly happy, even though their people looked upon them as outcasts.

However, there were brief periods when the Gros Ven-tres appeared to waver in their stubborn banishment of Wolf. When the first steamboat came up the Missouri River, several of the older men visited Wolf without enter-ing his painted lodge, his repeated warning against trad-ing with white men impressing them until conferences with their fellows in the village reassured them that there could be no danger from white men. And again, in 1866, when all summer a veritable procession of steamboats heavily laden with freight and white passengers churned noisily up the river bound for the rapidly growing town of Fort Benton, many of the older men smoked with Wolf, freely acknowledging their consternation, without inviting him to move his painted lodge to the village.

Soon after this, visiting Pecunnies and occasional Flat-heads told the Gros Ventres of great villages of white men that were in the mountains westward, speaking with awe of the number and sudden coming of whites there. This seemed incredible, even to Wolf, who, most of the time alone on the plains, pondered deeply over these tales. His dream seemed to discredit them, since the plains had not suffered by white men's passing. The buffalo were as plentiful as ever, and if many white men had reached the mountains, they must have traveled across the plains, leaving no desolation behind them. He did not guess that in their greedy haste to plunder the gulches the gold miners had virtually leaped from civilization to the Rockies, scarcely noting the grasslands. Secretly searching for the least sign of the passing of white men, Wolf saw no change on the plains; and yet tales of white village builders depressed him. His heart would not sing.

The following winter was fiercely cold, deep snow driving the horses into the cottonwood groves to browse, scarcely a day passing that the women did not have to chop ice on the river to get water. In Wolf's lodge, often wrapping an extra robe about her spare shoulders, Small-voice continually fed the fire. "I am an old woman, my son. My blood is lazy," she smiled, one bitter night when Wolf, noticing her withered hands in the firelight, tied an extra lining back of his mother's bed.

"No," he laughed, "you are not yet an old woman, Mother. You, like the rest of us are older than when—when Breath-feather and I ran away." Glancing at Breath-feather, who had grown noticeably heavier, Wolf wished that he had not spoken.

"Yes, Wolf, all of us are older. Soon I shall be too old to have children," she sighed.

And Wolf, who dearly loved her, looked down at his hands, covertly turning their backs to the firelight. "All things grow old," he said, simply. "Perhaps the day will soon come when we shall be glad that we are childless, my heart-woman." And here again was prophecy, since he could not have known that the fulfillment of his medicine dream was so nearly at hand, that already the white wasters were moving westward, and that even a conjurer would be powerless to picture the grasslands when they had passed. Indeed, there were visible reasons for the belief that the fulfillment of his dream's prophecy was far off. The buffalo were more plentiful than ever before, immense herds sweeping across the northern plains. He could not know that, constantly harassed by greedy skin hunters on the southern ranges, the herds were being driven to the north-western grasslands and that, when they were gone, the buffalo would come no more.

When finally the summer came, Wolf somehow learned that the white men had gone to war with the Sioux and Cheyennes over gold in the Black Hills, the mountains of the plains far eastward from his lodge. Twice during the summer the older Gros Ventres smoked with Wolf, talking happily of the war. "It is good," they declared, passing the pipe. "Let the Lakota die; let the Cheyennes die. They are our enemies. The white men are not disturbing us."

"No, it is not good," said Wolf, passing the pipe. "I hate the Sioux and the Cheyennes as you do, as we all do, but they are red men, as we are. If the white men wipe out the Sioux and Cheyennes, we shall be the next. You have forgotten my dream. The white men are coming, and we shall perish. My dream has told us this, and yet we have not listened."

But even when a little later Wolf watched the great Nez Percé Chief Joseph lead his desperate people in his marvelous flight across the norther plains to Snake Creek, where he surrendered to General Miles, Wolf, himself, saw no immediate menace to his beloved grasslands. The white soldiers went away, taking Joseph with them. The white men had changed nothing, disturbed nothing. The plains showed no mark of their passing, excepting the rifle pits on Snake Creek; and Joseph had dug these the better to fight the white soldiers. Wolf, noting all this, and the plenty that was visible on every hand, thanked his Helpers, The Winds, beseeching them to withhold punishment from his stubborn people.

Chapter 25

Wolf, perhaps by the "*moccasin telegraph*,"[1] had learned of Crook's defeat by the Sioux on the Rosebud, and Custer's annihilation by the Sioux and Cheyennes on the Little Bighorn, as soon as these bloody battles had been fought on Montana's southeastern plains, marveling that neither had in the least affected his people or the Pecunnies. But within a year after the capture of Joseph on Snake Creek, in spite of the continued abundance of buffalo, he became aware of listlessness, a letting down that had affected not only himself but the Gros Ventres and the Pecunnies. Their young men no longer organized war parties. There had been no attack by Crows or Sioux for two years, and during all this time there had not been a single horse-stealing raid, either by the Gros Ventres or against them. The tribes of the northern plains seemed to Wolf to have gone to sleep, excepting their women, who, without rest, dressed buffalo robes for trading with the white men at Fort Benton. Holding fast to his resolution to be of service to his weakened people, Wolf had faithfully pitched his painted lodge near the Gros Ventre village. Now there was

---

[1]Because the plains Indians seemed to be able to receive and transmit messages through thin air and over long distances, the white plainsmen coined the name "Moccasin Telegraph" for the mysterious method.—F. B. L.

no longer need for this. His people, despite his service, which the older men recognized, had not relented. He had given up all hope of reconciliation, of ever being invited to pitch his lodge in the village which he had guarded for so many years. In September he moved his lodge to the Marias, intending to spend the winter on the Missouri, his mother and Breath-feather looking forward to possible visits with other women in the Pecunnie village which might be somewhere near the Marias.

One late afternoon as he was idly watching buffalo, Wolf's attention was attracted to the peculiar actions of a large bull that appeared to be unable to keep up with the slowly moving herd. At each step the animal's head was drawn sharply downward as though tied to its foreleg near the hoof, as plainsmen sometimes tie saddle horses. Upon his approach the herd stampeded, the crippled bull fiercely turning upon Wolf, who killed the animal, his following examination astonishing him. Never before had he seen wire, and yet here was wire, barbed wire, many yards of it wound tightly about the animal's body, about the neck, back of the head, and around one foreleg. So deeply had the torturing strands cut into the flesh that they were entirely hidden, the hideous wound beneath the bull's foreleg exposing the bones of the brisket. As he was driven with his fellows from the southern ranges, the flimsy fence of some cowman had failed to stop or turn this bull. And as he tore his way northward, the barbed wire had attached itself to his heavy coat, tightening its hold about his body, its sharp barbs eating into his flesh until he could go no farther.

The seeming frailness of the metal strands which had enmeshed the huge buffalo bull astounded Wolf, who saw in them the first sign of the white man's coming to the northern grasslands. Here at last was evidence that his dream was true, something that could be seen and handled, a thing which would interest the Pecunnies. Using his horse to roll the huge carcass over and over, he laboriously unwound the wire, ripping it from the embedding flesh, yards of it, heavily caked with hair and blood, dragging it behind his horse to his lodge on the Marias. And here, a week later, a small party of Pecunnies examined it, their hands upon their mouths in astonishment.

But now, as though in defiance of the omen of the barbed wire, the buffalo blackened the plains along the Marias, the size of the herds tempering even Wolf's fears until one serene morning in October, which reminded him of his first flight with Breath-feather, he saw reenacted in flesh and blood a scene of the tragedy which The Winds had first shown him in his medicine dream.

Cautiously rounding a knoll on the plains to get the wind of a herd of buffalo, he was stopped in his tracks by the report of a heavy rifle. Its nearness, between him and the herd, was disconcerting. Intent upon his stalking, he had seen no hunters, and yet they were here. Climbing a knoll, looking down its other slope, Wolf saw a bearded white man lying prone upon a ledge of rock, hidden from the nearby herd by a single screening bush.

Drawing backward so that only his head showed above the knoll's summit, Wolf saw the white man, loading his heavy Sharps rifle from a well-filled belt of cartridges at his right hand, send shot after shot crashing into the dazed herd, watching the stricken buffalo stagger, sinking to their knees while reloading his weapon. Each shot stirred the whole herd, making the buffalo more uneasy until, bewildered by the noise of the rifle, they began to mill slowly, bulls and cows stopping to smell the blood which was pouring from the wounds of their dying compan-ions. But scenting no enemy, seeing only the spurts of smoke from the white man's rifle, the milling slowed down, many buffalo stopping to look about, their noses smelling the breeze. Not until thirty lay dead upon the plains did the herd stampede, racing madly northward, leaving the bearded white man on his *stand* with his *kill*.

Peeping from the knoll's summit, Wolf saw the killer rise, place his hat upon his rifle's wiping stick, waving it as a signal. Looking toward the Marias in the morning sunlight, Wolf saw a white man's wagon drawn by four horses coming toward the knoll, carrying four white men. Behind the wagon were two saddled horses. The bearded skin hunter did not wait for the wagon to reach the knoll. Hurriedly buckling his heavy cartridge belt about his waist, he ran to meet it, mounting one of the saddle horses to gallop northward in search of another grazing herd of buffalo.

Now the four men left their wagon near the *kill*, hastily ripping the skins of the dead buffalo down the bellies and legs, their keen knives severing the hide around the neck, back of the head of each animal, all of them working frantically, often two men on one buffalo until the thirty had been thus crudely prepared for skinning. While two of the skinners were ripping the last of the buffalo, the other two hastened to the wagon, returning to the *kill* with a team of horses, a heavy sledge and a *deacon*.[2] Driving the *deacon* through the head of the nearest buffalo into the ground, these men hooked the team's doubletree to the skin at the neck and then, starting the team, literally tore the hide from the animal's body with many pounds of clinging fat and flesh, repeating this performance until the thirty buffalo had been stripped of their robes, many of them badly torn. Unless they were promptly removed, the cling-

[2] A sharpened iron stake.—F. B. L.

ing fat and flesh would spoil the robes, and because such wantons as these spent more time in boasting of the size of their *kills* than in caring for their robes, many thousands did spoil and were utterly lost.

Wolf, fearfully fascinated by this terrible demonstration of the truth of his medicine dream, was transported. Covering his eyes with his hands, he saw himself sitting again on the cliff's edge, felt the Winds, saw again the strange yellow light in the sky, the darting, fiery arrows, the whitened bones of buffalo scattered over the desolated grasslands, heard again The Wind's warning. And then, as though suddenly awakened from his original dream by heartless reality, far off toward the north he heard the roar of the white man's heavy rifle sending death into another herd of buffalo.

Sickened by the realization that he would live to see the prophecy of his medicine dream fulfilled to the uttermost, Wolf saw the four blood-bespattered skinners hastily load the thirty mutilated robes into the wagon, driving away toward the sound of the killer's rifle, leaving the *kill*, nearly forty thousand pounds of fat meat for the wolves.

"O Winds, my Helpers, strike them down," he whispered, his legs trembling. But the white men had come to the grasslands. Like Wolf himself, the Winds were powerless. They could not help him now.

Unwavering in his fatalism, as are all the Indians of the plains, Wolf, like the others, was practical nevertheless. Here was meat, plenty of good fat meat. He would take it, saving all that he could of it for use. Next morning, with four travois, he and the two women began stripping the meat from the carcasses, first selecting the cows, vying with feasting wolves that would not leave the vicinity of the *kill*. Never before had Small-voice and Breath-feather dried so much meat at one time. Wolf, now fearful of want, worked with them until they had saved enough of the meat to last more than a year.

Moving to a comfortable grove of cottonwoods beside the Missouri, they pitched their lodge for the winter, the sounds of rifle shots often reaching them even there. Wolf, closely herding his horses, now more than thirty head, avoided the open plains, wincing at every rifle report that came to the grove as though he felt the impact of a bullet. The wanton slaughter of buffalo and their ruthless skinning constantly in his mind, Wolf found it difficult to appear cheerful in the lodge. His mother, no longer able to withstand heavy toil, showed the effects of their hasty work with the meat, her condition worrying him and Breath-feather.

While the winter was yet young, wolfers, white men, who were even more irresponsible and ruthless than the skin hunters, traveling in carts, appeared on the plains. Following the skin hunters, these men poisoned the meat of the dead buffalo to kill the wolves, their wind-swept camps littered with the frozen, hideously grinning carcasses, often sites of drunken revelries. Twice before the winter was half-gone, bearded wolfers stopped at Wolf's painted lodge, offering to buy pemmican or dried buffalo meat. Wolf, needing the meat, had refused to sell, both times by signs making it plain that he would feed the white men if they were hungry. These approaches by white men, who had been arrogantly insistent in their attempts to obtain the meat, worried Small-voice. The wolfers were continually traveling; their carts, drawn by teams of horses rolling over the plains, were often in sight. Knowing the value of dried meat to those who are constantly moving, and fearing that the abundance in their lodge might lead to trouble with these white men, Wolf's mother proposed

that most of their dried meat be cached in the cottonwood grove away from the lodge. Wolf and Breath-feather,
largely to satisfy Small-voice, who was suffering with a
lame back, agreed to this with the understanding that they
should make the cache themselves under her direction.
Carefully wrapping nearly three-quarters of the dried
meat in a section of discarded lodge skin, Wolf and Breath-
feather placed it upon a pole scaffold in a cottonwood tree,
the long bundle closely resembling a dead human body,
Small-voice chuckling at the analogy. "Nobody will think
of stealing that for food," she laughed. "I shall have to forget the shape of that bundle before I can eat the meat myself," she added, turning back to the warm lodge, now
thoroughly pleased.

There had been but two light snowstorms. The plains
were yet nearly bare; the snow in the cottonwood grove
where the trees shaded it was in thin patches, crusted
hard. In making their cache of meat, Wolf and Breath-
feather had been careful to leave no trail, avoiding the
snow patches between the lodge and the selected tree,
which was deep in the grove and up the river a little way.
But they need not have been so careful. By morning a thin
skift of new snow had covered everything.

A week later, while hunting deer in the grove up the
stream from the lodge, Wolf crossed the trail of a wolfer's
cart. The wheel tracks coming from the grove to the plains
were plain, the horses' hoof prints fresh in the light snow.
Instantly thinking of the dried meat, Wolf took up the cart's
tracks, back-trailing them into the grove to the tree of the
cache. The dried meat was gone, stolen by wolfers.

To follow the wheel tracks would be madness. Wolf
knew that, with their long-range rifles, the white men
would shoot him down upon sight. The winter was little
more than half gone. The loss of meat staggered him, his

thoughts turning to Breath-feather and his mother. They would be frightened, terrified, but they need not know for a little time, anyhow, perhaps not until they had used the dried meat in the lodge. In the meantime he would try to replenish his store of meat. Scarcely a day passed that he did not hear the rifles of the skin hunters. He would find another *kill* and take the needed meat before Breath-feather and his mother learned of their loss.

Chapter 26

Late in the afternoon, bringing in a small deer to the lodge, Wolf pretended happiness. He even sang, at last declaring that they needed fresh buffalo meat. "In the morning I shall look for a herd," he said, lighting his pipe.

He did not call upon his Helpers, the Winds, to help him find a *kill* of the skin hunters now. There was no need to disturb them. The frosty air of the plains was foul with the sickening odor of decaying buffalo. In every direction defiant wolves grudgingly left half-eaten carcasses lying in groups of ten to one hundred as he approached. But always the meat, the little left upon the bones, was too nearly putrid. Near midday, overjoyed by the sight, he found the carcass of a huge old bull lying alone in a coulee. The buffalo had lately been killed and hastily skinned. The fall before such meat would have been rejected as worthless. But now Wolf gladly cut a portion from the bull's carcass, tying it to his saddle. There would be time to carry it to the lodge, get Breath-feather and a couple of travois and bring the bull's meat to camp before night.

But the meat of the old bull was never brought to the lodge. While Wolf and Breath-feather were out catching the horses, making ready for their work on the plains, Small-voice, hungry for fresh buffalo meat, roasted and ate a small steak she had cut from the portion which her son had brought from the coulee. Returning to the lodge with the horses, Wolf and Breath-feather found her writhing, dying in agony, her last words warning them of the meat. It had been saturated with strychnine by the wolfers to kill wolves.

Stunned, their hearts torn by this sudden, fearful blow, Wolf and Breath-feather knelt beside the dead woman, the travoised horses straying upon the plains. Neither spoke. Neither wailed. Their grief choked them. They seemed scarcely to breathe. These three had been so long together, so long alone, so long and so unjustly banished from their people that their association had seemed immortal. "Gone," Wolf whispered, when the night had fallen. "Our mother has gone to *The Sand Hills*. Someday we shall find her fire there, my heart-woman."

Together they put the body of Small-voice in a cottonwood tree near the great river, the manner of her passing seeming to them to have been sent from another world. That night, alone in their lodge, they sat together for hours without speaking, watching their fire as they had so long ago watched the cheerful blaze in their new lodge in the Gros Ventre village. Now, as then, wolves were howling on the plains. But tonight their voices were different; the desecrated plains were different; Wolf and his woman were different. They were growing old.

"They cry," Breath-feather whispered, her graying head upon Wolf's shoulder.

"Yes," he answered softly, his arm about her, "they cry. The wolves cry."

"For the buffalo they cry," she said softly, as though whispering to the fire.

Much as he needed meat Wolf dared not take any from the *kills* now; and living buffalo were scarce, wild, difficult to kill with a bow and arrow. Now that Small-voice had gone, the dried meat in their lodge would last a little longer. Wolf, hunting deer in the cottonwood groves along the river, thought of this with bitterness. Perhaps, if he avoided eating much of it himself, the dried meat might last until spring, if he could find a few deer. But early in March, when deer were lean after the winter, he met good fortune in a grove beside the Missouri, killing a wounded buffalo that had wandered from the plains to die among the trees. This was the last buffalo for Wolf and Breath-feather. Even the elk had quit the plains forever. The following summer, except prairie dogs, offered little meat, roots, and berries to help Wolf and his woman to live.

And now another winter came. Snow, driven by blizzard winds, was piled about the plains, the coulees drifted full. And yet, despite the cold and snow and biting winds, the white hunters relentlessly followed the rapidly thinning herds until not a buffalo was left alive on all the northern grasslands.

During the hundreds, perhaps thousands of years of the Indian's occupancy of North America, the herds of buffalo had steadily increased until the red man's camps and villages were often in danger of being trampled into dust by the moving millions. That the Indian often killed more buffalo than he needed is unquestioned. Nevertheless, under him the buffalo had always increased in number. Now they were gone. Eight years before, in their northward drift, the herds were often twenty, sometimes fifty, miles wide and of unknown depth. Three years before, soldiers were sent out from Fort Keogh, at Miles City, Montana, to split a herd of buffalo which threatened to overrun the post. Now on the northern range where millions had roamed, not a buffalo remained alive.

Throughout this terrible winter starvation and death

stalked across the now pitiless grasslands. The Indians of all the tribes, so suddenly deprived of the buffalo, pitched from overplenty to direst want, died by hundreds, the Pecunnies, occupying the northern end of the Great Plains where altitude lent wicked power to the bitter winds and stabbing cold, suffering most of all.

Wolf and Breath-feather, camped alone on the Missouri thirty miles below Fort Benton, fared better than the others. But when the sage hens strutted again on the young grass, when the curlews returned, when the plain's rose mingled its loveliest of perfumes with the stench of rotting bones, Wolf wondered if there would be meat for man on the plains. The antelope, greatly thinned in number, constantly frightened by the buffalo hunters and wolfers, were wild, difficult to kill with a bow and arrow. There were fish in the river. But what Indian of the northern plains would eat fish, *The Under-water-people?* None. Twice during the winter Wolf had killed deer in the river bottoms, their skins furnishing many pairs of moccasins. Thanks to Breath-feather and Small-voice they still had plenty of buffalo robes.

Springtime, with its marvels, came on as though nothing had happened, driving the drifts from the coulees, carpeting the plains with velvety green. But now, where the buffalo had wallowed and wandered for centuries, bulls, cows, and calves of another breed began grazing as though the buffalo had never been. The white man's cattle had come to the *cow country*, "the best summer range on earth." Wolf, first seeing these spotted, multicolored creatures on the plains, believed that they had been supernaturally sent to replace the buffalo, but not for long. White men were always near the cattle, white men who shot at every wolf, every antelope, and coyote as though the grasslands belonged only to themselves. Wolf, who had occasionally killed antelope, could not get near them with his bow and arrow now. His dried meat had long ago been finished. He knew that Breath-feather, like himself, was sometimes hungry. The cattle tempted him, and yet, because white men were near them, he dared not kill a cow. Earlier in the spring, when their store of meat was dangerously low, he had found a wolfer's horse dead on the plains. The animal had stepped into a snow-covered badger hole and broken its leg. The wolfer had shot the horse, leaving it unskinned and therefore unpoisoned, where it had fallen. The horse had been shod, its iron shoes, the first that he had seen, exciting Wolf's curiosity. But the horse was thin, nearly skin and bones. Besides this, Wolf had divided its meat with a starving Pecunnie so that it had not lasted long.

To near exclusion of other food these Indians had always been meat eaters. When one understands that the dried meat of a buffalo cow weighing twelve hundred pounds will not weigh ninety pounds and that the daily ration of dried meat issued by the fur companies to their engagees was three pounds per man, he will realize the red man's constant requirement of meat. Wolf, unable to find meat, led one of his horses to camp and butchered it. Now, with roots, bulbs, and berries, saving as much meat as possible, Wolf and Breath-feather began to live on their horses.

When fall came, the most beautiful time of year in the Northwest, a new lure had attracted white men to the plains. The foul-smelling bones of the exterminated buffalo were gathered by a motley crew, who trundled them to the new, far-off railroad in rickety wagons and Red River carts. The bone gatherers brought another menace to Wolf and Breath-feather. Twice, while Wolf was hunting for deer in the river bottoms, in their efforts to seduce her, these white men offered food and even money to Breath-feather, who, frightened by their licentious, bearded faces, fled to Wolf for protection.

"We will move," Wolf told her, struggling with his swift anger. "We will move down the river where I may find deer in the groves. We will select a place away from the plains and winter there, my heart-woman. We will go today, now," he finished, gently quieting her fear.

But when Wolf went out from the lodge to drive in the horses, they were gone, stolen! That morning, and each day, as Indians do, Wolf had visited the band, thirty head of good horses. Now they were gone. In a moment he had found their trail. Within another moment he had found the imprint of a horse's iron shoe, an iron shoe like those on the wolfer's dead horse. White men had stolen his horses! Even if he had dared, he could not follow the thieves afoot. Realization of his loss, like an icy hand upon his heart, left him weak, unnerved, afraid that Breath-feather would die of hunger. "O Winds," he whispered, lifting his harried face. But The Winds did not help him. Their potency had passed with the buffalo herds.

Even though in a brave effort to shield Breath-feather, Wolf told of their loss with forced laughter, a new, a horrid dread sat between them and their fire that night. "There are rabbits," Wolf said, as though suddenly remembering the meek among animal kind. "Tomorrow I will hunt rabbits, be a boy again. We shall be lovers," he laughed, selecting sinew for snares.

Sobbing, Breath-feather, unbeguiled by his acting, put her arms about his neck. "You have been kind to me, always kind. I love you, Wolf," she whispered. And Wolf, to save himself from showing weakness, his utter helplessness, rising, left the lodge.

The fall, as though reluctant to make way for waiting winter, lingered until rebelling north winds wrathfully drove it from the plains. Wolf, hunting in the river bottoms, setting rabbit snares among the bushes, eating rose hips to save meat, saw the storm's first warning. Turning to go back to the lodge with his rabbits, he heard a rifle shot in a grove not far down the river. Believing that some wolfer might have killed a deer there and that the hunter might leave the animal's head and its entrails, he made his way to the grove, stopping at its edge, where the tracks of a wolfer's cart entered among the trees. Listening, Wolf heard low voices beyond the bushes bordering the grove. Indianlike, the instinct to learn what these white men were doing among the cottonwoods, to see without being seen, urged him to steal through the bushes until he could look into the grove. Not far from the river two white men were busily butchering a fat yearling steer. Their team, hitched to the cart, was tied to a small cottonwood nearby. Tethered to the rear of the cart, a saddled horse browsed upon nearby bushes, his flanks wet with perspiration. Wolf knew that the white men had used the saddle horse to drive the steer into the grove from the plains.

Working swiftly, scarcely speaking now, the white men skinned and dressed the beef, severing the head, quartering the carcass with an axe. And yet, because he knew that the steer belonged to white men, Wolf suspected no wrongdoing here, even when he saw the wolfers cut a large patch from the steer's hide, tie a stone to the patch, and throw it into the river. He could not know that this discarded patch of skin bore the owner's brand and that its removal would render positive identification of the remaining hide impossible in the white man's courts.

The coming storm was bending the tops of the tall cottonwoods in the grove when the two wolfers loaded the quartered meat into their cart, covering it first with a wagon sheet and then with freshly taken wolf skins, lashing it securely with ropes. And then they were gone. Wolf could not believe that they had intentionally left the hide, the liver, the heart, and the head. Surely when they noticed the absence of the liver and heart, they would return for them. Climbing a tree, the fierce wind lashing his hair, Wolf saw the cart going steadily eastward across the stormy plains. The cold was growing intense. The steer's hide would freeze. Descending the tree, Wolf severed the useless lungs from the mass, slit and emptied the bulging paunch, and then with the already stiffened hide and willows he made a sack for the entrails. The head could wait.

Dragging his heavy sack, Wolf was singing lustily above the gale when he reached the lodge. "Meat, Woman," he called, panting at the uplifted door. "Meat, Woman," he repeated his eyes merry when Breath-feather stepped outside.

"The rabbit hunter has returned to the village. Now you have work to do," Wolf said, hastily explaining his good fortune. "I'll go back for the head," he told Breath-feather, leaving her to empty and wash the entrails in the icy water of the Missouri.

Fine, gray-looking snow that stung her face was lashing out of the north when Breath-feather, having stripped and cleaned the steer's intestines, hung the hide across a pole near the lodge, carefully straightening the skin so that it might freeze without wrinkles. Here was needed rawhide for moccasin soles. Her hands were stiff and numb, her face smarting from the stinging snowflakes when, thinking of Wolf carrying the steer's head through the storm, she kindled the lodge fire.

Its first smoke had scarcely reached the howling wind outside when Breath-feather heard horses near the lodge. Frightened by her experiences with wandering white men, she cautiously peeped through a slit in the door. Two young white men, cowboys astride their horses, were minutely examining the steer's hide on the pole, furtively glancing at the lodge. Breath-feather saw one of the cow-boys point mysteriously at the jagged hole in the hide where the owner's brand had been cut away, saw the other nod understandingly; and then both men rode away, their heads bent low against the biting wind.

Chapter 27

Throughout the night the shrieking blizzard tore at the tops of the cottonwoods. All night the snow whirled in sheets about the lodge, the steer's head, with its glassy, staring eyes freezing solidly within the door.

At dawn, the storm abating, Breath-feather kindled the lodge fire, remembering that having prudently emptied her paunch kettle the night before she would have to go to the river for water. Wolf, awakening, sat up to look across the crackling fire at the steer's head. "If we sleep a long time, we shall not have to eat so much meat," he said seriously, his breath white in the frosty air.

"Anyhow, we shall need water," said Breath-feather, going out with her kettle. Stopping to look at the steer's hide, she saw that coyotes had been about the lodge in the night. "Everything is hungry now," she sighed, wading through the drifts toward the river.

Wolf listened to her crunching steps in the dry snow. Could he feed his woman until spring came again, he wondered. When summer came, could he then find meat? The bears did not eat during the winter. They slept. He would sleep. He would pretend that he was not hungry.

The following day, the weather continuing bitterly cold, Wolf was sleeping, or pretending to sleep, when a team of horses stopped at the door of the lodge. "Come out here, damn you," growled a white man, thrusting his head and shoulders through the door, a cocked six-shooter leveled at Wolf. "Come out o' that," he commanded, this time beckoning impatiently.

Staring in bewilderment at the bearded face in the doorway Wolf understood only the man's gesture. "Lie still. Do not feel afraid," he said evenly to Breath-feather, his hand on her shoulder. "I will go outside," he told her, snatching up a robe.

Passing the door of his lodge, he was seized by two white men, roughly handcuffed, and then loaded bodily into a waiting buckboard. "Better take that critter's hide along with him," one of the men said, pitching the frozen skin into the rig behind the seat. "The dirty red devil was smart enough to cut out the brand," he chuckled, climbing in himself. "All set, Tom?" he asked, picking up the reins. They were off, heading toward Fort Benton, nearly thirty miles away, the half-naked Indian wedged tightly between their burly bodies, comfortably clothed with heavy buffalo overcoats.

Hearing her screams, Wolf turned his head to see Breath-feather racing after the buckboard, her hair streaming wildly, a naked knife in her hand. "Go back," he called. "Keep your fires burning. I will return," he promised, watching the terrified woman stop in the snow, covering her face with her robe.

"That was easy," said the driver reflectively, flicking the horses with his whip.

"Shore! Shore! I ain't never seen an Injin yit that would fight a settin' hen," sneered his companion. "They ain't no good, none of em, an' they never will be. If our fool gov'ment hed the sense that God give to bedbugs, it would order out our lazy soldiers that never earns their salt and make 'em shoot down every damned Injin they come acrost. They'd make bait for the wolfers; that is, if a decent wolf would eat a dirty Injin. Set *over*, damn ye!" he ended, bunting Wolf's lean hips with his own. "Bet ye're lousy as a pet coon. I don't want to git 'em, damn ye!"

The snow was not deep on the plains. Even though there was no road, the buckboard, avoiding drifts, traveled rapidly, the horses white as the snow with frost. Hungry to weakness, the stabbing cold tortured the patient Indian. His bare wrists, encircled by icy steel, seemed to chill the blood in his arms and hands. Understanding no word of English, he could not guess why these men had taken him. He did not know where he was going. Thoughts of Breath-feather's plight, her terror, her scanty supply of meat, her danger from heartless wolfers were worse than his hunger, worse than the cold. And he was powerless, helpless as a rabbit. Even The Winds had forsaken him now.

Near ten o'clock that night, when the stars seemed actually to snap in their brilliant sparkling, Wolf, his handcuffs removed, was pushed into an iron-barred cell in the jail at Fort Benton. "There, damn ye, think it over an' git warm," laughed the man who had talked most on the way from the lodge. "Come on, Bill," he said to the driver, "let's us go down to Murphy's an' git us a hot toddy: and then let's swaller a fat beef steak apiece before we bed down, hey?"

On the wall, across from Wolf's cell, a single coal-oil lamp burned, its wick turned low, its chimney grimy with soot. In the near corner a pot-bellied stove, a round, red spot the size of an apple on its bulging side, warmed the room. Somebody was snoring. Wolf had heard this snoring even while the men were locking him in his cell. Now, when the men were gone, besides the snoring there was singing, swearing, ribald conversation between cell and cell. These men must have been seized, taken as he had been taken, or they would not be here. He was not alone. Everybody seemed to be good-natured, happy enough in their confinement. If only he could speak to them, ask them why the white men had taken him away from his woman, what they would do with him! He would try. "Ho!" he called, warmed by a feeling of fellowship. "Can any man here understand the Gros Ventre language? If he can, let him speak to me. I am lost."

His weird, chantlike sentences coming so suddenly in the half-lighted jail gripped the other prisoners as the voice of a village crier must grip any white man. The snoring stopped. The jail was so silent that Wolf could hear the fire crackling in the stove. No man replying, Wolf spoke again, this time in Pecunnie, his heart leaping when he was answered from the shadows at the far end of the room, from the cell of a French trapper who had been awakened from sleep by Wolf's voice. Speaking more rapidly, Wolf now told his story to the unseen friend who had been jailed for drunkenness, the other prisoners, fascinated by the strange speech of both men, listening in silence until they had finished.

The long winter night in the stuffy, overheated jail, tortured by fear for Breath-feather's safety and his own need of food, was a terrible ordeal for Wolf, who had never before been in a house of any kind. Watching, intently listening to every footstep, every sound outside as a wild creature suddenly caged and helpless must listen, Wolf saw the first streaks of dawn, heard the jailer enter, saw him first stir the fire in the stove and then walk straight to the cell in the far corner of the room, his keys jingling in his hand.

"Mornin', Frenchy," the jailer said, unlocking the cell door. "Awful cold this mornin'," he went on, giving the

French trapper advice. "I put you in here last night to keep you from freezin' to death. Mind yourself today. It's awful cold. If you git drunk an' fall in the street, you'll sure as hell freeze. Now, git out o' here, Frenchy. An' git you some breakfast before you start drinkin' again."

Laughing good-naturedly, the little Frenchman shook hands with the jailer. "Some day you come my camp," he invited, dancing the Red River Jig, his moccasined feet fairly flying. "Bon jour," he waved, stopping a moment at the door of Wolf's cell to speak briefly in Pecunnie before going outside.

The jailer, having replenished the stove, followed the trapper out of doors, leaving the fire burning briskly. The other prisoners, awakened by the Frenchman's laughter and dancing, began to talk, to grumble, two hours passing before the jailer came again, this time not as the lord of all creation but as a menial in the presence of a king. Seizing a broom, he began industriously to sweep the jail floor.

"Come here, jailer. Let this Indian out so that I can see him" ordered a white-haired man, stopping beside Wolf's cell with the Frenchman and the driver of the buckboard.

"Yes, sir, Judge," bowed the jailer, opening the cell door.

"Now, Frenchy, tell the Indian why he was arrested," the Judge said, turning Wolf so that the light of the early morning sun fell upon his face.

The Judge, watching Wolf's eyes as the Frenchman spoke, saw them light with sudden understanding, saw the Indian's tense muscles relax, as only innocence could have relieved them. When Wolf, who had waited, as an Indian always waits, until the trapper had finished, launched himself into the story of the steer's death, the Judge stopped him. "Tell him I know his story," he said. And then, turning to the driver of the buckboard he asked, "Did the court issue a warrant for this man's arrest?"

"No, your honor," the driver said. "You see, it was this-a-way. The cow outfit told me that this Injin had killed a steer of their'n, told me where he was camped, and said they'd seen the hide there. They didn't know this Injin's name. Nobody did; so I, me and Tom, went out an' got him."

"And the hide, minus a brand, is all the evidence you have against this man?" asked the Judge, a little severely.

"Yes, your honor," admitted the driver. "The hide and the head. It was in this Injin's lodge."

"You are to make no more arrests without warrants from the court. The Territory has no money to waste. Let this Indian go. He's discharged," the Judge said. "Thank you, Frenchy," he added, shaking the trapper's hand before leaving the jail, followed by the buckboard's driver.

"Well, I'll be damned if you ain't got a pull with the Judge, Frenchy," laughed the jailer, pitching his broom into a corner.

"Oui," grinned the trapper, handing Wolf a small sack containing boiled beef. "De Judge, she's know I'm tell de troot, me. She's damn smart man, de Judge. Come," he said in Pecunnie, turning to the wondering Indian, leading him outside.

"Now you go to your woman," he told Wolf, watching the Indian start down the river on a dog trot, eating from the sack.

"He's a Gros Ventre, is he?" asked the jailer, watching Wolf disappear over a hill. "An' Gros Ventre's French ain't it?" he asked.

"Oui. He's mean *beeg* belly; but dat man she's got damn *leetle* belly. She's hongry lak hell, dat man."

Everybody in Fort Benton knew honest, irresponsible Frenchy. Within an hour after Wolf had left the jail, the little trapper was drunk, would remain drunk until his hard-earned money was gone. Then, following his rough vocation, he would betake himself to the wilderness and alone set his traps until he had gathered enough fur to pay for another protracted spree.

Wolf, with nearly thirty miles to travel afoot in the sub-zero weather, scarcely felt the cold. Cutting straight across the plains for his lodge, he stopped only once to drink sparingly from the frozen river when it bent out to meet his course. Not one living creature had he seen on the plains when darkness came. But when at last his eyes made out the lodge at the edge of the grove, there was no fire burning in it. Trotting faster, weary and worried by the dark lodge, he began to sing, calling playfully to Breath-feather to show a light, his heart bounding when a flickering flame answered.

"Here, Woman, eat," he laughed, bursting into the lodge with the half-filled sack of meat which the Frenchman had given him, his rapidly told story so filled with merriment that the woman believed he had been well treated and bountifully fed.

Chapter 28

Even though Wolf had been careful to pretend differently to Breath-feather, his arrest had frightened him. Realizing that now, with the charge of cattle killing already against him, white cattle thieves would find it easy to fasten their further crimes upon him, he was secretly anxious to move the lodge to the badlands down the river, to hide in that man-forsaken section and to somehow find a living for his woman there. He felt that he had been lucky in Fort Benton, that the little French trapper had perhaps saved his life; and yet he wondered what his life was worth to him now. If he could have been assured that Breath-feather would have meat after he had gone to *The Sand Hills*, he would have welcomed death. But there could be no such assurance. He must avoid a second seizure by white men and feed his woman. He must move to the badlands.

For hours after the lodge fire had burned out, he lay quietly in his robe, his mind busy with his problem, the loss of his horses seemingly insurmountable. If the great river had been open, he might have easily made a raft with drift logs and let the water carry Breath-feather and himself and their meager property down the stream. But the Missouri was frozen solidly from bank to bank, and a sled would leave tracks in the snow for the white men to follow.

Nevertheless, he decided that he would build a sled and travel on the river's snow-covered ice until he found a satisfactory site for the lodge. He would leave the lodgepoles standing where they were, taking chances upon finding others down the river. The tracks of the sled would not last long. The first snowstorm would wipe them out. The white men might not try to find him before the next snowfall; after that he could feel safe since there was nothing for white men in the badlands, nothing at all; and there would be little enough in that weirdly broken country for himself and his woman.

At daybreak Breath-feather listened delightedly to Wolf's plan, eagerly wading with him through snowy willow thickets in search of sled material. At her suggestion they made two sleds instead of one, being careful to gauge their runners so that those of the second sled would fit and follow the other's track, binding the willows into sled form with thongs cut from the green skin of the steer's head.

"Ho, Woman!" Wolf laughed, carrying the finished sleds into the lodge after the fourth day's work. "Our work is finished. Now build up a good fire. Our rawhide lashings must dry a little before we use these sleds," he said, setting their creations on their ends against lodgepoles, carefully examining their handiwork in the bright light of the fire.

But the sleds were never used. The news of Wolf's arrest for cattle killing had reached the ears of the Indian Department's agent at Fort Belknap, nearly seventy-five miles down the river from Fort Benton, as the crow flies. White cowmen could vote. They must be protected from the depredations of nonvoting red rustlers. "Bring in the cattle thief," were the orders issued by the Indian agent, so that by the middle of January, Wolf and Breath-feather had pitched their tattered lodge in the deep snow at Fort Belknap.

They were not entirely ignorant of the fate of their people. They had heard, through the Pecunnies, that when the buffalo had been wiped out the soldiers of the Great White Father in Washington had gathered the Gros Ventres and Assiniboines at Fort Belknap under the promise that the United States government would feed and clothe both tribes. Hearing this, Wolf had pitied his people, smiling skeptically at the White Father's promise, not once believing that he, an outcast, could have any part in these strange arrangements. He was growing old. The Winds had forsaken him; and yet, afraid of *Those Who Live Without Fire*, he had no thought of offending them by seeking needed aid from white men. Now, against his will, he was here, virtually a prisoner and utterly friendless. Even though Left-hand had been dead for nearly twenty years, every Red man on the Belknap reservation knew the story of Wolf and Breath-feather, all of them, even the Assiniboines, believing that Wolf had brought the *bad sickness* to the Gros Ventres. They shunned him, passing him in the deep snow without even a glance, their whisperings so exciting their little children that they peeped furtively through covered lodge doors to catch glimpses of the bad man whose misdeeds had long ago brought disaster to his own people.

Quick to catch the feeling of fear which his coming seemed to have brought to Fort Belknap, well knowing that the scourge of smallpox and the nearly thirty years which had elapsed since he and Breath-feather had left the Gros Ventres to live alone on the plains had taken all who might now have befriended them Wolf understandably, kept aloof from his distrustful tribesmen. But worse than all this, perhaps to placate the dissatisfied, grumbling Indians of both tribes, or perhaps because they believed that he had stolen cattle from white men on the plains, the authorities on the Fort Belknap Reservation gave Wolf and Breath-feather scanty attention, leaving them to shift for themselves after issuing their first meager rations. This issued food was strange to Wolf and Breath-feather. They did not know how to prepare it. Flour and beans! "How can we live without meat?" Wolf wondered. But there was scarcely any meat. Wolf had already heard strong men beg for meat at the agency office, had seen these beggars tramp back through the drifted snow to their lodges bearing nothing but empty promises for their hungry women and children. Men who had horses killed and ate them. Wolf had no horses, not even a dog; and because they believed him guilty of having brought the plague to the tribe, he could expect no help from the Gros Ventres.

Distrusting the white men at the agency, whose promises were as thin as the winter air, fearful of the integrity of the White Father in far-off Washington, Wolf from the beginning had carefully conserved the rations which had been issued to him and Breath-feather, constantly denying himself to make them last for his woman. But the food was disappearing, and at the agency there was nothing to be had excepting vague promises.

Desperately hunting rabbits each day in the snow coulees where there were now too many hunters, eating rose hips, fearful that Breath-feather would starve to death, Wolf evolved a plan to save her. He knew that she had not been deceived by his abstinence from food, knew too well that she had often lied about her eating, as he had lied about his own; but now, unless the white men at the agency were deliberately lying about the coming of food, he could save his woman by pretending that he had made a friend of the White Chief at the agency office and that this white man secretly fed him there.

His return to the lodge was after darkness had fallen.

Tossing a single rabbit at Breath-feather's knees, he heaped dry wood on the fire. "Ho, Woman, I have eaten too much," he laughed, merrily rubbing his famished stomach. And then, kneeling, he told his story, his tired eyes lighted by the love in his heart. "I will go there again tomorrow and the next day and every day until our meat comes to us," he whispered across the bright lodge fire.

Breath-feather believed this story; and Wolf began his pretended visits to the agency, merrily refusing to share the miserable food in the lodge until, four days before help came to Fort Belknap, the last morsel was gone.

Then, one bright morning when Breath-feather was kindling her fire, a bobsled with jingling bells stopped outside the lodge, leaving a shoulder of beef and a sack of flour in the snow there. "Wolf! Wolf!" she called, lifting the door in the dazzling sunlight; "Wolf! We have meat, meat! The white men have brought us meat, Wolf," she said, creeping excitedly across the lodge to Wolf's robe.

But Wolf did not waken.

Wolf and the Winds,

designed by Bill Cason, was set in Palatino by G&S Typesetters, Inc., and printed offset on 55-pound Glatfelter Antique by Cushing-Malloy, Inc., with case binding by John H. Dekker & Sons.